Touching the Moon

TOUCHING
THE MOON

John Preston

HEINEMANN : LONDON

William Heinemann Ltd
Michelin House, 81 Fulham Road, London SW3 6RB
LONDON MELBOURNE AUCKLAND

First published 1990
Copyright © John Preston 1990

A CIP catalogue record for this book
is available from the British Library
ISBN 0 434 60260 4

The extract on page 74
from *On the Road* by
Jack Kerouac is reprinted
by permission of André Deutsch Ltd.

Printed and bound in Great Britain
by St Edmundsbury Press Ltd, Bury St Edmunds, Suffolk

For my mother
and for William and Cathy
with thanks for everything

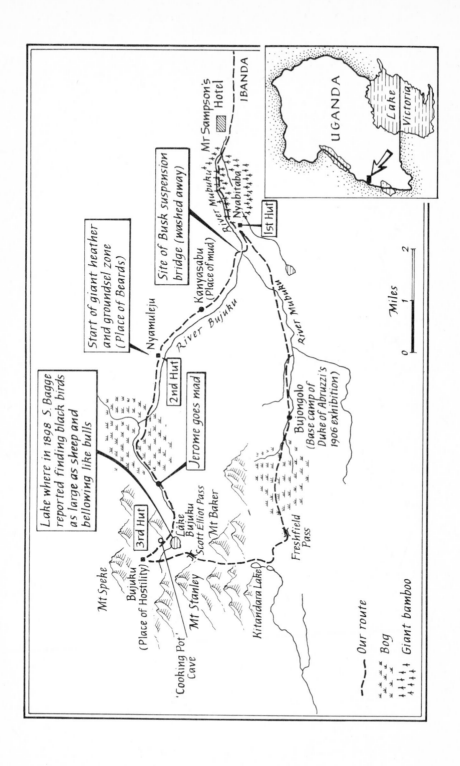

Lake where in 1898 S. Bagge reported finding black birds as large as sheep and bellowing like bulls

Start of giant heather and groundsel zone (Place of Beards)

Site of Busk suspension bridge (washed away)

Jerome goes mad

Mt Speke

Bujuku (Place of Hostility)

'Cooking Pot' Cave

3rd Hut

Lake Bujuku

Mt Stanley

Scott Elliot Pass

Mt Baker

Kitandara Lake

Freshfield Pass

Bujongolo (Base camp of Duke of Abruzzi's 1906 exhibition)

River Mubuku

Nyamuleju

2nd Hut

River Bujuku

Kanyasabu (Place of mud)

River Mubuku

Nyabitaba

1st Hut

Mt Sampson's Hotel

IBANDA

UGANDA

Lake Victoria

Miles
0   1   2

———— Our route
ᴧᴧᴧ Bog
↟↟↟ Giant bamboo

One

My grandfather had a box which he kept in a cupboard in his study. It was battered and peeling and covered in maroon leather that had faded to pink in places. Strips of hide hung down around the sides as if the thing had been flayed. Occasionally my grandfather would take the box down from its shelf and show me what was inside. Special indentations had been made in the satin lining to hold the contents. It was full of objects my grandfather had picked up on his various foreign postings in the army. I don't think there was anything particularly valuable in there; they were simply bits and pieces that had caught his eye.

There was a thorn twig from the Mount of Olives, bleached white by the sun and so brittle that it had to be handled carefully for fear of it crumbling away. A piece of chalk from a quarry in Kurdistan was wrapped in brown paper. An opium pipe from Singapore was laid alongside. Below each item was a typed note giving details of where it had come from and the circumstances of its discovery. My grandfather was a very meticulous man. Here too was a square of purple cloth that had once been part of a robe belonging to the Sultan of Oman. The explanation of how my grandfather had come by this was unusually vague – no date was given, any enquiries were always waved away. I used to imagine my grandfather being ushered into the royal presence in some tented desert palace and surreptitiously snipping the material from the Sultan's hem as he knelt before him. It was an exciting scene – acquisitiveness triumphing over awe in the middle of nowhere.

The box fascinated me. I would implore my grandfather to open it up. But he knew how to mete out these favours so that the anticipation never palled. Sometimes the moment was right, sometimes it wasn't. The box also revealed a new side of my grandfather's character, a side that otherwise was kept well under wraps. Behind a rigid, rather stern exterior he had a strong fascination for the exotic.

I was never in any doubt that this was a dangerous liability. My grandfather always brought forth the box with an air of subterfuge, as if there was something shameful about the whole business. My grandmother was always out or a safe distance away. She would not have approved. The message was clear enough. A fascination for the exotic had to be kept rigidly under control, otherwise it could spill over and cause all sorts of havoc, threatening decorum, stability and all the other pillars of respectable family life. It was an important lesson.

My grandfather kept two pigs. There was nothing odd about this, apart from the fact that he couldn't bring himself to kill them. Both were well beyond the point where they could be eaten, having passed into ungrateful dotage. One had long white whiskers that hung down either side of its snout. The older they grew, the more bad tempered they became, and the more they resented any sign of human life. They were kept in a pigsty up beyond the north wall of the kitchen garden. It was their own private domain where they stomped about in their own muck and bellowed at any visitors. You could hear them from the other end of the village. Few dared to venture there. Feeding them was like feeding tigers – you had to throw shovelfuls of food over the wall of the sty and run for cover.

The only other discernible eccentricity in my grandfather was his habit of growing his own tobacco. This was regarded as harmless, but none the less odd. My grandmother had to endure a succession of foul, acrid smells round the house as my grandfather experimented with various home-made solutions for soaking the tobacco leaves. Sealed drums of Senior Service cigarettes, obtained at special concessionary prices from the local Naafi, were left stacked up untouched in his study, alongside the maroon box.

I used to sit and watch as my grandfather hung the huge leaves from lines of baling twine strung across the loft. The loft was above what had once been the stables, but any horses had long since gone. Gardening implements rusted away in the hay troughs, shelves of cooking apples decayed in the stalls. The smell rose up through the floorboards – rich and rotten. Getting to the loft entailed climbing a vertical ladder bolted to the wall and undoing a trapdoor. When the trapdoor swung back on its hinges a dry rustle ran through the loft as the tobacco leaves shifted and crackled on their lines.

Kept separately from my grandfather's box, but always brought out at the same time was a tiny book, hardly bigger than a matchbox and bound in the same maroon leather. It was called *The Pleasures of Hope* and had been written in 1820 by 'A Friend' to Miss Anne Carswell. The book was full of poetry written in a minute crabbed handwriting. My grandfather and I would peer through a magnifying glass and read out passages to one another. I was very taken with the opening lines:

> At summer even, when Heav'n's aerial bow
> Spans with bright arch the glittering hills below
> Why to your mountains turns the musing eye
> Whose sun-bright summit mingles with the sky
> Why do those cliffs of shadowy tint appear
> More sweet than all the landscape smiling near?

The book was a love token. It must have taken years to write. There were a few poems written by Byron, but most seemed to have been composed specially. Towards the end the writing got thicker and less neat, as if the writer's sight was going, or the Pleasures of Hope had finally evaporated.

My grandfather and I used to speculate on how the gift had been received. Neither of us could drum up much optimism for 'a friend's' chances. My grandfather thought there was a possibility that all his work might have swayed Miss Carswell's heart. I, however, thought it very unlikely. Why was I so adamant about this? I was only ten years old. And yet somehow I knew that he had blown it. Rather than being smitten by the strength of her suitor's affections, Miss Carswell would have been appalled. The man was a hopeless obsessive, maybe even dangerous. I saw her leafing horrified through the pages. He had gone too far, tried too hard. The very thing he had been banking on had scuppered his chances. In one respect, though, I felt he had

3

got it right. It was hard to understand just why, but things far away really were a lot more attractive than those close at hand.

At much the same time as I discovered the secrets of my grandfather's box I started reading Rider Haggard. All the other books I had ever read immediately faded into complete insignificance. Here at last was proof that somewhere out beyond the kitchen garden and the pigsty, lost civilisations lay undiscovered, hidden riches were buried in great vaulted caverns and immortal queens bathed in fire. The news came as a big relief. I was beginning to have my doubts. But no, it was all right. It was just a case of knowing where to look.

Rider Haggard's heroes always knew exactly where to look. Decent, unexcitable types, usually weighed down with pervading melancholia, they had an extraordinary knack of attracting various maps, ciphers, scarabs and other clues which kept turning up unbidden at their bachelor apartments. Decipher the hieroglyphics, find the Hill of the Skull, skirt the mountain the natives call The Finger of God, and you were away. Everything hung on getting hold of the right talismans.

My grandfather's box, I realised, was full of them. Mysterious objects from remote places with a story attached to each. This realisation signalled a rapid change of perspective. From sitting enraptured while my grandfather told me of his exploits, I quickly progressed to a starring role in each adventure. The box was the spur, Rider Haggard provided the substance. There I was, neatly attired in buff fatigues and bush hat, snooping round the opium dens of Singapore, lowering myself into Kurdistani quarries, sharing a quick joke with the Sultan of Oman before whipping out the pinking shears and setting about his robe. All the while picking up clues that led me onward, ever closer. Towards what? I had no idea where the trail led, what lay at the end of the line. There was only one requirement. It should be something even stranger and more fantastic than King Solomon's Mines. Something to make the dullest imagination stand up and yelp with astonishment.

My favourite by far among the Rider Haggard books was *She*. It has nothing like the pace or sustained excitement of *King Solomon's Mines*. Nor is it as good as its sequel *Ayesha, or the Return of She*, which has what must surely be one of the greatest opening lines in literature: 'Verily and Indeed it is the Unexpected that Happens.' But there was something about *She* that made me read it again and again. Perhaps it was the eroticism. Rider Haggard, while taking a predictably dim view of actual physical contact between men and women, was not above the odd bit of discreet voyeurism. 'The white robe slipped from her down to her girdle baring the divine loveliness of her form.' I tried constantly to imagine just what form her divine loveliness would take, but it was difficult. I had very little to go on.

Here too I learned for the first time of the full horrors of death, as She or Ayesha, having waited 2,000 years for the reincarnation of her lover, leads him into the eternal flame that will assure them both everlasting life. But something goes terribly wrong. She has been overdoing the heat. Her metabolism just can't take it anymore.

Age, kept at bay for so long, suddenly, appallingly, catches up with her. One moment She is bathing quite happily in the flames. The next, she reaches up to touch her hair and it falls off. This was undiluted horror. You casually flick back a stray forelock and your entire scalp drops off on to the floor. Reading this in bed I would stuff large portions of blanket into my mouth to muffle my whimpering.

And there was worse to come. The flesh soon begins to wither on her bones, puckering up and blackening in the heat. Her hands become talons, her chest caves in, her legs give way. Within a matter of seconds there's nothing left, She has crumbled to dust. So this is what you had to look forward to. Until then I had thought of adults as being able to do anything they chose, unfettered by rules or people telling them how to behave. It was my first inkling that there might be a price to pay for this. I also brushed my hair with enormous care afterwards, never pulling too hard at the tangles or putting any undue pressure on the roots. The risks were much too great.

Even so, *She* still became a blueprint of the way I hoped my life would go. I wondered which of the book's two heroes I would end up resembling most. It was a difficult and stark choice. There was Leo Vincey. Young, almost impossibly handsome, strong, brave, irresistible to women. An outdoor type through and through, but a definite underachiever when it came to anything academic. While

Rider Haggard doesn't quite say as much, it's clear that Leo can barely write his own name without assistance.

Or there was his loyal friend and guardian, Horace C. Holly. By contrast, Holly's brain is in excellent shape, but it's just about the only part of him that is. As he himself says – Holly shows a perverse relish for listing his failings – 'Like Cain I was branded with the stamp of abnormal ugliness.' Cain at least had a psychotic temperament to go with his looks. Holly, however, is cursed with an exceptionally gentle and selfless disposition. Not that it does him much good. Even the men in his Cambridge college don't care to be seen with him. As for the women, they grimace with alarm and scuttle by on the other side of the road.

So which was it to be? Leo or Holly? The problem was that I seemed to be stuck somewhere in the middle. There was no evidence at all that I was impossibly handsome. Neither was I particularly clever. It was tough enough trying to be average. The only other possible role-model was their manservant Job, a reliable enough factotum, but quite colourless and without any of the wisdom of his Biblical namesake. Maybe that was it then. Maybe I was fated to be one of nature's Jobs, forever lugging around Gladstone bags and complaining about the state of the gentlemen's shirts.

Age plays tricks on memory, usually cruel ones. I grew up convinced that *She* was set in the Mountains of the Moon. This was where She Who Must Be Obeyed ruled over a lost tribe in the Kingdom of Kôr and where anyone who stepped out of line was thrown into a vast pit bristling with sharpened stakes. In the 2,000 years spent waiting for Leo to come back She has developed quite a taste for this. Not a great reader, nor much of a one for hobbies generally, among the few things that stops her from brooding is consigning large numbers of the population to the big pit.

I had no idea where the Mountains of the Moon were supposed to be, but the name stuck in my mind. It was redolent of everything that appealed about Rider Haggard: mysterious, remote and unearthly.

Rereading *She* again not long ago I waited patiently for some reference to the Mountains of the Moon. There was nothing. I went through it again. A complete blank. I couldn't understand it. It was like rereading *Wuthering Heights* and finding that Heathcliffe has vanished from the narrative. Something had gone badly wrong here. I'd begun to think I must have dreamed the whole thing when, one Sunday afternoon, I switched on the television and saw the opening credits of *She* (Hammer 1965) roll up on screen. And then I remembered.

At school we had weekly film shows. The films picked were almost always either old Will Hay comedies or war films – naval ones were considered superior to any other kind. We sat in rows in the gymnasium and watched attentively enough as men in duffel coats stood on conning towers and scanned the horizon through binoculars for signs of enemy presence. There were bursts of cheering, led by the deputy headmaster operating the projector, every time a German ship was hit. Twenty years after VE Day the memory of war was kept carefully kindled. Up on the South Downs where we were sent on runs, trenches had been left cut in the ground in case they might be needed again.

We were warned not to have anything to do with the foreign language students who could be seen walking disconsolately along the seafront during the summer. There was apparently a danger that they might offer us sweets. Most were French or Belgian, but that made no difference. Being 'Continental' was sufficient grounds for suspicion. The world outside the school grounds seemed to be one where guttural voiced strangers tempted small boys with pieces of chocolate and toffee. I used to wish they would. They never did.

The cinema in the town was strictly out of bounds – lots of strangers, plenty of confectionery, all manner of temptation. But one Saturday I went by myself to see the afternoon matinee of *She*, which had been released a few months earlier. It was every bit as good as I had hoped. I marvelled at the splendour of the sets, thrilled once again to the power of the story and fell helplessly for Ursula Andress. It was my first grand passion for someone who was not aware that I existed. But at eleven years old I did at least realise that the pleasures of hope could not seriously be entertained. Like She and Leo, Ursula and I were victims of bad timing.

Watching the film again I rocked back and forth in disbelief. It was terrible. Shudders ran through the Kingdom of Kôr whenever someone brushed against a pillar. Peter Cushing's Horace C. Holly lacked anything approximating to abnormal ugliness – no plummeting widow's peak, no simian jawline. Leo Vincey was a peroxide beach-boy. The performance of Bernard Cribbins as Job did nothing to raise my spirits. Could this really be the same film? But there was Ursula Andress, not aged a day. (So that much at least was true.) The white rayon of her dress still pulled taut over her breasts.

And there too was the answer to my confusion. Embarked on their quest, the three travesties go, for reasons never explained – it corresponds to nothing in the book – to Arabia. There they meet up with a very Home Counties belly dancer, hire some camels and set off into the desert. On the outskirts of town, pointing away from a cluster of cardboard houses, there is a sign stuck in the sand. It reads, 'Mountains of the Moon' with an arrow pointing off to the right. No mileage is given.

One weekend in December 1964 my parents came to see me at school. I was eleven. It rained as it invariably did, and we walked up and down the seafront, past the pitted turquoise bulk of the Esplanade Hotel, whiling away the hours between lunch and the beginning of Alan Freeman's *Pick of the Pops*. There were no foreign language students around at this time of year, only windswept geriatrics, hauling themselves along the railings, hand over hand. The town was full of old people and boys' prep schools; there was scarcely anyone there between the ages of thirteen and seventy. All available folds between the cliffs were crammed with tiny retirement bungalows. Occasionally, on our school walks, we would run into another straggling convoy coming in the opposite direction, made up of wheelchairs and people on Zimmer frames. We passed without any sign of recognition.

The waves were cascading over the seafront with even greater ferocity than usual and so we turned inland. I was aware that something odd was going on. My mother was nervous, my father hardly said a word. As we were walking past the cinema – showing Burt Lancaster in *The Train* – my mother told me that my grandfather had died.

The news made no impression on me at all. At the time I was

obsessed with getting hold of a miniature cricket bat, about 6 inches long, with the autographs of the 1964 Australian cricket team printed on the face. Hearing of my grandfather's death only increased my determination to have it. Presumably to cushion my feelings, or else taken aback by this rampant consumerism, my parents bought it for me. Afterwards, a long time afterwards, I thought I saw how grief can occasionally manifest itself in flights of acquisitiveness. I wondered too if I had instinctively begun plugging the gap left by my grandfather's death by accumulating strange objects of my own. It seemed only faintly plausible. The more I thought about it, the less likely it seemed.

It was only later that evening that the news hit me. I wept uncontrollably in a mood of growing astonishment. It was like some reflex action I had no control over. The next morning the headmaster told me I had been suffering from delayed shock. I was surprised but pleased. To be suffering from shock at all was prestigious enough. Somehow the fact that it had been delayed made it all the better.

Soon afterwards I had another brush with death. This was heralded in an unusual way. It was my last year at the school. As a special privilege senior boys were allowed to go swimming naked during the summer term. No one thought this in the least bit odd. We would get up half an hour earlier than anyone else, take off our pyjamas, wrap towels around our waists and run in Indian file out to the swimming pool. The headmaster would be leaning against the filtration unit, one arm thrown out across the creosoted cover in a pose of exaggerated calmness.

We hung up out towels and lined up by the side of the pool, approximately a yard from the water's edge. The ritual was simple enough. The headmaster would walk down the line between us and the pool, hands clasped behind his back, eyes fixed on our groins. The general theory was that this was so he could check up on our pubic growth, if any. Most boys, including myself, were still quite hairless. One boy, however, was already showing signs of extraordinary hirsuteness. His testicles were covered in a thick black mat of hair, great tufts stood up on his shoulders like epaulettes. When he swam it looked as if he was wearing a cloak. He was persecuted relentlessly for this and in time took on an ashamed, guilty look as if he deserved everything he got.

When the headmaster reached the end of the line, he would turn and pat each boy lightly on the bottom. Whereupon you took two steps forward and did a little swan dive into the water.

One morning we got up as usual and ran out to the swimming pool. The headmaster was there waiting, but it was clear that he had something else on his mind. He was distracted. The pubic inspection was a cursory affair, he scarcely gave our private parts a second look. There was a mood of some indignation among the boys. We jutted out our hips petulantly, but to no avail. Bottoms were tapped without enthusiasm as we fell artlessly into the water. Something was wrong.

At prayers the headmaster rose and lent on his lectern. He stared at the floor for some moments before announcing that Winston Churchill had died during the night. The school immediately went into frenzied mourning. The Union Jack was lowered to half-mast on the flag pole, a memorial service was announced. 'This is a black day for England,' we told each other. The more adventurous boys speculated on the effect Churchill's death might have on national morale. The news affected me deeply. Once again I started crying, this time with hardly any delay at all. As I did so I had a nasty feeling that it could prove awkward in later life if I was to burst into tears every time I heard someone had died, irrespective of whether I had known them or not.

I asked the matron how old Churchill had been. She was a large woman with forearms about the same circumference as my thighs. We were queuing up for spoonfuls of malt extract in the dispensary. The malt was supposed to strengthen our bones and fortify our constitutions. She plunged the long steel spoon into the jar.

'He was a good age,' she said.

I lay in bed wondering about this. How could a man clearly in a state of hopeless decrepitude be reckoned to be a good age? And what did that make me? There was only one possible answer. I was a bad age, with long decades of unrelieved depravity to look forward to before some distant prospect of salvation.

Churchill's funeral was an occasion of great excitement. Lessons were cancelled for the day. Televisions had been brought in specially and connected up round the assembly hall so that we could all have a good view. On the screen Richard Dimbleby launched into his long oration. Outside on the gravel the headmaster's old black Labrador mounted the deputy headmaster's boxer dog. It was a protracted operation entailing several attempts and signs of impatience from the boxer. I didn't know where to look; my interests were cruelly divided. As Churchill's cortège made its way slowly down Whitehall to the beat of muffled drums, the buttocks of the headmaster's Labrador began to pick up speed.

At the end of term we took a special school train back to Victoria. The atmosphere, as always, was jubilant. We loosened our ties and looked at the emergency stop chain in various states of temptation. Some kind of grand gesture seemed called for. I debated with myself for a few moments then threw my cap out of the window. I watched as it was carried away, tumbling and turning in the wind before falling by the side of the track. There was further cheering. I was congratulated on my irresponsibility.

Soon after the beginning of the next term I was called into the headmaster's study. Two men were standing there in dark grey suits. One of them had a clear polythene bag with something green in it. It was my cap. They were policemen. The headmaster said that my cap had been found at the scene of a robbery near Hayward's Heath, and asked how I had come to lose it. I stumbled my way through a very unconvincing sounding account of how I had stuck my head out of the train window forgetting that I had my cap on.

The policemen nodded. They announced that I was not under suspicion of being involved in the robbery, although they believed that one of the thieves had been wearing my cap. I was astonished. For a start the cap was so small that it could only have been worn by another child, or a dwarf.

The headmaster asked if I might have the cap back. 'I'm sorry sir,' said one of the policemen. 'This is now a piece of evidence.' I was told that I could go. As I was opening the door the other policeman said, 'I would just warn the young gentleman that he shouldn't go sticking his head out of railway carriages whether he's got a cap on or not.'

'Quite,' said the headmaster. 'Very good advice.'

There was never any further mention of the incident. Even so, there seemed all sorts of lessons to be learned here; about discarded things coming back to haunt me, and about my basic unsuitability for impulsive gestures. Meanwhile, somewhere in Sussex, there appeared to be a boy with my cap size who had fallen into a life of larceny and danger. I envied him.

I wished I could be like the boy thief. Almost as much as I wished I could be like my great imaginary superhero, Demetri Diege – pronounced to rhyme with siege. I cannot remember when I invented Demetri, or when he stole into my life. It's as if he just turned up one day, fully formed and ready for action. Demetri was a spy, constantly engaged on work of pressing national importance. I drew pictures of him all over my exercise books and revision papers. He was small, with an enormous nose – somewhat similar to W. C. Fields's, but naturally bulbous rather than distended by alcohol.

Demetri dressed in a manner that, for me, embodied his attractions. An olive green combat jacket on top, with a purple ballet dancer's tutu beneath. This was Demetri's trademark and one that struck terror into his adversaries. He was fearless, of course, but with a neat line in self-deprecation, any impulse towards pomposity being defused by the every-present tutu. He was someone with a clear understanding of the absurdity that often lies beneath heroic gestures.

Demetri starred in a series of adventures. Rider Haggard was always the inspiration, the Mountains of the Moon the favourite location. Here was a place infused with all the excitement I could imagine. I thought of huge, snow-capped mountains linked by a tracery of hanging bridges and tiny paths. There were great fortresses rearing up into the clouds, dark pools where men in armour drank long draughts of inky water, plateaux where armies thundered back and forth in perpetual combat. Above all there was Demetri. I would imagine him abseiling down walls on fraying ropes, tackling hosts of crazed swordsmen, and leaping from pillar to parapet with a sure-footedness that owed much to his ballet training. Demetri was everything I was not. I wanted desperately to be adventurous and intrepid, but I simply wasn't cut out for it.

In time I began to feel that I'd had enough of Demetri. The gap between us was too great. He and I were worlds apart. One night Demetri went off on an adventure – I'd begun to wonder if he was capable of anything else. The dangers were piled up higher than ever before. The air was heavy with foreboding. He packed his things and left with that curious flouncing walk that so many had scorned, to their eternal regret. The next night I waited in vain for news. And the next. I tried to visualise what had happened. I saw only a bridge over a stream with some broken wooden railings and signs of scuffling on the ground. Demetri did not return.

Under the conditions of my grandfather's will his maroon box passed to me. This news prompted deep apprehension. Without my grandfather's help, I doubted the power of my imagination to make the contents come alive. One day my grandmother asked me to come and pick up my inheritance. I took it up to my bedroom, hearing the contents rattle inside as I climbed the stairs. *The Pleasures of Hope* had been wrapped up separately in brown paper. I sat down on my bed and opened the box. It was just as I had feared. The objects in the box were no longer keys to adventure. Now they were merely a collection of things like any other things. There was even something faintly embarrassing about them. I put the box away.

Years later I found it again. Everything was still there. I took out the thorn twig from the Mount of Olives, forgetting how fragile it was. It crumbled to dust in my hands, just as She had done in the great chamber of Noot where 'the fire of life roars like all the thunder-wheels of heaven behind the horses of the lightning'.

Two

Perhaps it is in childhood that imagination transports you furthest of all. Only then is the unknown quite so beguiling, the mysterious so dark and inexplicable. Only in childhood can you create another universe so freely, people it with whoever you want, and disregard any natural law that gets in the way.

I believed in the Mountains of the Moon. They were somewhere I could retreat to when the going got rough, beyond the reach of untrustworthy friends and enemies. I had only to shut my eyes and swallow hard. And with a faint plop like a body being pushed through a membrane. I was there. In the Mountains anything was possible. Heroism got its just rewards, meekness was nothing to be ashamed of – I was hedging my bets here – and caps once jettisoned never returned.

It couldn't last. Things changed. I grew up. Rider Haggard was left untouched on the bookshelf. The Mountains faded from view, and my taste for adventure shrank into some dark recess. A brief series of incidents accelerated the process.

I was almost twenty, living in Bristol and working as a van driver delivering electrical supplies around Somerset. One of the other drivers was a man in his late twenties called Leon. He was very thin and had that habit – common, as I was to discover later, among a particular breed of egomaniac – of talking so quietly he could hardly be heard. His voice seldom rose above a whisper. You had to go into all sorts of contortions to hear what he was saying, sacrificing a good deal of poise in the process and being left with nagging worries about possible deafness.

One morning I was walking across the yard carrying lengths of copper piping when Leon indicated that he wanted to talk to me. He did this in a strange manner, flapping a hand to and fro in a desultory sort of way while half turning to the wall as if he had confidential news to impart. I hurried over. Wisps of streaked blond hair hung over his collar. An animal tooth dangled from one ear. Leon claimed it was a tiger's tooth although it looked more like it had come from a dog to me. It turned out he wanted somewhere to live.

'Can you help me?' he whispered.

There was nothing plaintive about this, it was hardly even a question. He looked at me expectantly. I was horribly eager to please. The house I was staying in at the time was rented by students, most of whom had gone away leaving instructions that their rooms should be sublet to anyone who expressed interest.

Leon came round that evening. He looked around with enthusiasm, agreed that it was better than living in a hostel and paid two weeks rent in advance. He moved in immediately. I asked if I could help him with his luggage. He frowned at me and shook his head. I watched as he climbed the stairs to his new room, his arms laden with carrier bags.

We had little to do with one another. Leon was not an easy companion, being enormously secretive about his past and lapsing into bemused silence if the questions were not to his liking. There was something disconcerting too about his laugh. It would rattle along mirthlessly for a while and then peter out, like a wraith slowly disappearing alongside.

One Sunday evening Leon arrived back at the house in a state of great excitement. He had on a new royal blue denim suit with cross-stitching round the lapels and was carrying two large suitcases. He beckoned me outside. There parked by the front door was a brand new red Ford Cortina. 'Mine,' said Leon. And that wasn't all. Up in his bedroom he opened the suitcases. The first was full of new clothes – twelve identical prewashed denim shirts, each inset with brass studs on the breast pockets, and several matching pairs of jeans. He laid them out carefully on the bed. The other suitcase was full of marijuana. There must have been kilos of it, packed in clingfilm. 'That's mine too,' said Leon.

'How did you get it all?' I asked. He gave no sign of having heard me.

Thereafter Leon became more sociable, offering me lifts in his car and asking my opinion about small variations in his wardrobe. Often in the evenings we would cruise down City Road where the prostitutes congregated under streetlamps and hoisted their skirts at the passing traffic. This became one of Leon's favourite pastimes. We would join the kerbcrawlers, proceeding in convoy at a steady 10 miles an hour. The prostitutes peered through the passenger window as I sat pressed back in my seat, grinning fixedly in a state of barely suppressed panic. Somewhere something had gone wrong. This wasn't the way I had planned to grow up at all. It felt as if Leon was Leo Vincey, and I his ugly sidekick Horace Holly in a world gone irredeemably to the bad.

Leon only ever stopped once. It was the moment I had been dreading. He told me to wind down the window. There were two women outside. One of them squatted down on her haunches so that her face was on the same level as mine. She had a little pink birthmark above one eye.

'Would you and your friend like to come to a party with us?' asked Leon.

'What?' said the woman.

He repeated the request.

'I can't hear you love,' said the woman. 'Can you speak up?'

Leon dug me in the ribs. 'You ask her,' he whispered.

It was as if invisible hands tightened around my epiglottis. I opened my mouth. Nothing remotely resembling words came out. Instead there was a sound like carbonated water coming to the boil. The woman with the birthmark began to look concerned.

'What's the matter with you two?' she asked.

The other woman came over. They stood on the pavement and tried to decide if we were foreigners or both troubled by speech defects. After a while they shrugged and walked to the car behind. Leon drove off at speed, his face set in grim profile as he hunched over the steering wheel. The episode was never referred to again.

Ever since Leon had arrived back with the car he had been spending money at a rate that amazed me. By now the walls of his room were covered in Chinese silk wall hangings, still more pre-washed denim shirts were scattered about in their wrappers. One weekend we drove to Blenheim Palace where the Rolling Stones were giving a party to launch their new record. Leon was convinced that we would be able to gatecrash the party without any difficulty. We stood and watched as circus trucks sped through the streets of Woodstock and in through the palace gates. There were security guards everywhere, local men recruited for the occasion and apparently ranged in concentric rings around the palace to intercept any intruders. In the pub there was even talk of their being issued with staves.

Leon was undeterred. I pleaded with him to reconsider, but it was hopeless. He looked at me with disgust. 'Haven't you got any taste for adventure?' he asked. I wanted to explain that I had an inexhaustible appetite for it on paper, but something odd happened as soon as it got tangled up with reality. My body ganged up on me. I was a walking compendium of self-betrayal. White flags streamed from every pocket. There was a little mocking voice that ran through my head at times like these. 'Into the valley of Death,' it chanted, 'Rode the Five Hundred and Ninety nine . . . Ti Tum, Ti Tum, Ti Tum . . . Someone had blundered.'

We climbed over the wall into the palace grounds and dropped into the undergrowth below. There were little clusters of light where the guards stood, smoking cigarettes. It began to rain. We ran out across the grass, diving into bushes and hiding in ditches at any sign of trouble. Leon was barely able to contain himself. In the dark his face glowed with excitement. I ran along at his heels, feeling that my intestines were uncoiling behind me in a long, luminous giveaway. After well over an hour we got to the main door of the palace. Both of us were covered in mud. Our clothes were sodden, our faces streaked with brown. Pieces of grass were stuck to our hair. There was a huge bell-pull by the door. Leon pumped it up and down. A bell jangled inside. A few moments later a man in full livery answered the door. He wore a powdered wig with a black velvet bow at the back and white leggings below his knee breeches. He looked at us without saying anything and then, with a tilting of his head, ushered us inside. We walked down a corridor, feet squelching on the parquet floor.

The corridor led into a ballroom. On the far wall was a portrait of the Duke of Marlborough inspecting his troops before the Battle of Blenheim. There was hardly anyone there. A few waiters hurried about clearing up plates and glasses. The last guests were in the process of leaving. The Rolling Stones, we were told, had left some time earlier. We asked a waitress if we could have a drink. She looked surprised and came back with two glasses of ginger ale.

'We made it then,' said Leon, showing no sign of disappointment.

When we had finished our ginger ale we gave the glasses to the waitress and walked back down the corridor. The footman opened the door and wished us good night.

At work on Monday morning we sat around eating sandwiches and drinking coffee that shot out of the vending machine at groin level in a boiling, horizontal stream. Someone asked Leon if he had had a good weekend. Leon became unusually animated, claiming to have had a very good weekend indeed. He started to give an account of our trip to Woodstock. This time, though, things had changed considerably. According to Leon we had evaded the clutches of several hundred men – armed with both staves and shotguns – before making it to the palace door. Fortunately, the party was in full swing when we arrived. Leon described the guests, the champagne, the delicious canapés, the hubbub of animated conversation.

'And did you get to meet the Stones?' he was asked.

Leon gave an apologetic smile. 'Not all of them,' he said.

Alas. Poor Charlie Watts, it transpired, had missed out on an introduction. As for the others, Leon grew steadily more expansive, telling of how he and Mick Jagger had discovered a natural rapport rare in its intensity. As for Keith Richards, Leon hinted at the discovery of distant bloodties, reprobate ancestors sprung from the wrong side of the same blanket. I listened to all this in astonishment. It was the most blatant piece of lying I had ever heard. What made it even worse was Leon's confident assumption that I would do nothing to challenge his story. As for the others, no one showed any signs of doubting what he was saying. When Leon finished there were gasps of wonder from the men who muttered, 'Well I never' in awed tones.

But afterwards my astonishment gave way to reluctant admiration. Leon's example was worth noting. It didn't seem to matter what had really happened to us at Woodstock. It was the telling that was important. Particularly the way in which Leon had made himself the hero of a hopelessly unheroic escapade. As long as you had sufficient imgination you could soon leave the truth behind and get on with the serious business of creating a personal mythology for yourself. Leon was evidently very accomplished at this. And I felt that given a little practice, I could get quite good at it too. Here was an ideal way of bringing reality into line with expectations. It was easy. All you had to do was create a plausible character and put it over with due conviction.

Over the next few days I began to experiment. I told of how I had been orphaned at an early age – plane crash, jungle, suggestions of cannibalism – and brought up on a Hebridean island where my closest companions were seals. It was extraordinary. No one disputed it, scoffed with disbelief or asked awkward questions. People's credulity may have had its depressing side, but it also offered all sorts of possibilities. I was exhilarated. The only thing to remember was to steer clear of situations where reality could trip you up.

One Saturday morning two weeks later there was a knock at the front door. Three men in raincoats stood on the step. One of them held up a card. I peered at it. There was a dim black and white photograph and some smudged print. 'Special Branch,' he said. Two of the men pushed past and ran upstairs, while the other held me against the wall. After a few minutes the two men came back downstairs.

'He's not here,' they said.

'Where is he?' said the man holding me against the wall.

'Who?' I asked.

'Leon Cavanagh.'

'I don't know.' When I looked down I could see the tops of his fingers pressed against my chest. They were yellowy white, as if the blood had drained back to his knuckles.

For the next hour I was interrogated about Leon. How long had I known him? Did we get on well together? Who were his friends? They knew all about the new car. One of the men laughed when he mentioned it. 'Leon's been naughty,' he said.

They all looked at me. I found the word 'naughty' oddly reassuring, suggestive of childhood misdemeanours rather than anything serious. Even so, as with the prostitutes in City Road, speech came awkwardly. 'How naughty?' I croaked.

A month beforehand there had been a bomb explosion in Hampstead Tube Station. The bomb had been timed to go off in the rush-hour, but the timing device didn't work properly and it exploded in the middle of the night when the station was deserted. An anarchist group called The Angry Brigade had claimed responsibility. Several weeks earlier they had bombed the flat of the Home Secretary. According to the policemen, Leon had driven the gelignite used in the Hampstead bomb up from Bristol to London. He was the only person who would take on the job because the gelignite was old and unstable and liable to detonate of its own accord. In return Leon had been paid with the car. But the car had been stolen, no one had even bothered to change the number plates.

'He may come back,' they said. 'If he does, get in touch.' One of them gave me a card. As they left, he wrinkled his nostrils and said, 'This house smells of cat piss.' There was no mention of the two suitcases.

Weeks went by without any sign of Leon. The chances of his coming back seemed remote. In the meantime, my supply of shirts was disintegrating fast. My elbows jutted through sleeves, buttons fell off, collars frayed. The thought of all those pristine shirts upstairs began to prey on my mind. One evening I went up to his room. His shirts were hanging in the cupboard. On the shelf above there was a bulky package. Inside was the manuscript of a novel written by Leon. It was enormously long, more than 400 closely typed pages. The opening line read, 'I am the choirboy who has found the golden rivet.'

The shirt I picked fitted perfectly. I thought of the boy thief who had worn my school cap and wondered if he could have possibly grown up into Leon. Now I was donning both their identities. For some reason I felt more guilty about wearing the second of Leon's shirts than the first. But I soon overcame it, and before long guilt had given way to irritation that Leon's shoes were half a size smaller than mine.

There was an easy downward slope from the clothes to the marijuana. A friend of mine and I opened the suitcase and stared at the remainder of Leon's cache. Little was left. What there was looked unappetising, large brown sticks like pieces of bamboo with hardly any foliage attached. The next day we bought the strongest parsley grinder we could find – it was a special catering model to cope with large loads – and set about grinding the twigs into a more acceptable state. It was hard work, some of them were like pieces of kindling. When we had finished a pile of chewed-up twigs lay on a polythene bag on the floor.

No one wanted to buy any. We dropped the price so often I felt as if we were on some sort of mercy mission. Even then people complained about feeling ill and demanded we return whatever tiny amount they had been charged. At last, only the stalks were left. I rolled them in newspaper and hid them under my bed. We counted up the meagre profit and agreed it had been a waste of time.

A few days later I got back from work to find a note had been pushed through the door. It was addressed to me and typed on lined paper that had been perforated in places by pressure on the keys. 'I know you've been wearing my clothes and selling my grass,' it said. 'I've got good reason to think you shopped me to the police. I'm sending down some people from London to sort you out. A shotgun blast at close range is a very unpleasant sight.' It was signed Leon.

I remember thinking that I had to be careful not to wet myself. I sat down on the bed in my room and looked at the note again. It was still exactly the same. So this was it, I thought. I was 20 years old and now I was going to die. It had been a life of thwarted expectations, and it was going to end in a manner as far removed from the heroic selflessness of a Rider Haggard hero as possible. I would be the smallest small-time drugs dealer ever to be murdered by a hitman.

I drove down to the central police station, my foot quivering on the accelerator pedal. The policeman behind the formica-topped counter looked bored. Beside me a drunk tried to fill out a form and swore at the difficulties involved. When I asked to speak to the name on the card I had been given, the policeman suddenly became more attentive. He went off to seek advice. Soon he came back and took me upstairs, to the top floor where there were carpet tiles instead of lino and brass light fittings on the walls.

I was shown into a room where two of the men who had interviewed me were sitting behind a table. They told me to sit down. I pulled out the letter from Leon and showed it to them. Neither said anything. 'It's all true.' I blurted out. One of them began to take notes. I was appalled to see I was wringing my hands. My involuntary gestures alone were enough to warrant a conviction. 'I don't know how I got myself into this,' I added.

The man who had held me against the wall shook his head. 'You've been very stupid,' he said. I nodded vigorously in agreement. And then, because they seemed to be waiting for me to say something, I told them all about the marijuana, the shirts, the shoes, the prostitutes, everything I could think of. It was like a massive purgation of all the untruths I had heaped around myself. The more I thought about it, the more I realised there were. I told them about the trip to Blenheim and my subsequent feelings about truth, invention and the fragility of the self – or my own self to be more exact. I saw the man taking notes shoot worried glances at his companion as I got into my stride. They even tried holding up their hands but I swept on regardless. There was a lot on my mind that I wanted to get rid of. It was tempting to tell them all about Demetri, the Mountains of the Moon, Ursula Andress and even my cap, but before I could get on to them the man sitting opposite told me to stop. He repeated it several times with an edge of desperation in his voice, as if he was addressing a train that was bearing down on him.

'I think you've told us enough, sir,' he said.

'But . . .'

'No, really. We have all the information we need.'

The two men consulted for a while in whispers. I sat back and stared up at the narrow cornice that ran round the walls. I remembered how C. S. Lewis had said that as a child he always felt God was gazing down on him when he looked up at the top left-hand corner of a room. Or was it the top right-hand corner? I couldn't remember.

The men stopped whispering and turned to face me. 'We've

decided to give you police protection for a few days in case anyone does come for you,' said the one who had been asking me questions. There was a long pause. No one said anything. Then, almost in unison, the two of them said, 'You can go now, sir.'

'But what about . . . ?'

'Do us a favour and throw it away will you, sir.'

I got to my feet. Somehow the air seemed thinner when I was standing up. My trousers had stuck to the backs of my knees. I was escorted downstairs and back to my car.

A policeman moved in the next day. He spent most of his time in the kitchen, cooking curried baked beans on the one working gas ring. After four days he left. The hitman from London never came. I never heard from Leon again.

On the night after the policeman left, I took the roll of newspaper containing the marijuana stalks from under my bed, hid it under my jacket and walked to the Clifton Suspension Bridge. It was a cold night. There was no one about. I walked out to the centre of the bridge. The lights of Bristol lay spread out before me. I took out the paper and shook the stalks out over the parapet. Thick white twigs dropped into the darkness below.

Three

Every weekday morning we would go to the British Museum Reading Room to write our novels. It was an arrangement doomed to failure from the very start. My friend Edward Cathcart and I would sit opposite one another beneath the great domed ceiling where every sound reverberated like gunfire. Figures sat hunched over the long, leather-topped desks that fanned out from the middle of the room like spokes in a cartwheel. We would open our pads of paper and set to work.

It was 1976. Neither of us had jobs. This though was of no significance. The important thing was that we were about to become Men of Letters. The way ahead was clear, the milestones already well marked. Initial promise, startling debut, critical acclaim, growing distinction, worldwide reverence, state funeral. But our trips to the Reading Room were not working out as I had hoped. What had begun in a mood of considerable optimism had become – for me anyway – a grim daily ritual. I was adamant that I wanted to be a writer. There was no doubt about this. But finding something to write about was proving much more difficult than I had ever anticipated. Character eluded me. So for that matter did plot. Every day I would scour my own experience for suitable subject matter. It was hopeless. I was 23 years old and nothing of any significance seemed to have happened to me at all. Emily Dickinson had led a more eventful life.

In desperation I had embarked on a story set in prewar Poland, unfettered by historical research or even a precise idea of where Poland was. The Polish cavalry figured prominently in the story. They rode aimlessly back and forth across vast swathes of turnip fields – dimly remembered from geography lessons – while I tried to think up something for them to do. This was going no better than any of the other novels I had started and then abandoned after a few

24

pages. I proceeded at the rate of about one sentence a day. They were not even particularly memorable sentences. Looking at the previous day's work was always a depressing business. My mood plummeted sharply from foreboding to despair as I read, 'The sun gleamed dully on their spurs in what was left of the late afternoon sun.'

Edward, on the other hand, wrote quickly, seldom looking up and cupping an arm round his sheet of paper to shield it from prying eyes. I would try and distract him, clearing my throat as loudly as possible or gasping for air in a manner intended to suggest that my windpipe was blocked. There was never any response. Everyone else in the Reading Room was also lost in concentration, oblivious to outside distractions. I was the only one stuck hopelessly in the here and now. My imagination seemed a dull, sluggardly thing, unable to transport me anywhere. I sat in front of my blank sheets of paper and gazed around in a state of envy that scaled new heights each day.

The knack lay in finding your subject. But nothing stirred me, nothing kicked me into life. Edward had plumped unhesitatingly for his subject: The Bomb. Quite what he was writing about the bomb was unclear – I didn't like to ask. But there was no doubt that he was on to something pertinent – books on the bomb had become a whole new literary genre. A new bomb had just been invented, one that destroyed people and left buildings standing. I, however, dreamed of something much more sophisticated. A bomb that would destroy every significant work of literature ever written. This seemed to be my only hope. Then in the post-holocaust age I could really come into my own, author of the only text to survive the explosion, now revered as sacred and recited with impassioned fervour by the survivors, 'The sun gleamed dully on their spurs in what was left of the late afternoon sun.'

One day when work was going particularly badly and the Polish cavalry was even more listless than usual, I picked up a book from the top of a pile left by the last occupant of the chair beside mine. It was a copy of *In Darkest Africa* by Henry M. Stanley. I leafed through it without much enthusiasm. Stanley had never been one of my favourite explorers. There seemed something pompous, worthy, offputtingly dogged about him, although as far as I could remember, I had never read a word he had written. I opened the book at an engraving of an elephant trying vainly to flee a hunting party, squirting water behind it as it ran up a river bank away from the gunmen who were in a boat moored alongside. Puffs of engraved smoke hung from the ends of their gun barrels. 'The Winchesters were worked handsomely,' noted Stanley in evident satisfaction.

But later on there was a passage that had me staring at the book with renewed interest. Stanley had written:

To hear about wonderful salt lakes that might supply the world with salt . . . of large-bodied Wazongora, and numbers of amiable tribes; of the mysterious Wanyavingi, who were said to be descended from white men; to be in the neighbourhood of colossal mountains topped with snow which I believed to be the lost Mountains of the Moon, to be in a land which could boast of possessing the fabulous fountains de la lune; a veritable land of marvel and mystery; a land of tall men and pygmies and tall men reported from old, and not feel a glad desire to search into the truth of these sayings!

He – the Maker who raised those eternal mountains and tapestried their slopes with the mosses, and divided them by myriads of watercourses for the melted snow to run into the fruitful valley, and caused that mighty forest to clothe it, surely intended that Africa should be reserved for something higher than to be a nursery for birds and a store-place for reptiles.

I had a momentary glimpse of Ursula Andress, her white dress still pulled impossibly taut over the jutting splendour of her breasts. I read on. Two days later, marching along just before sunset, Stanley and his men had seen the mountains again, through a brief gap in the clouds:

Soon after 5pm the upper extremities of those spurs loomed up one after another, and a great line of mountain shoulders stood out; then peak after peak struggled from behind night-black clouds into sight, until at last the snowy range, immense and beautiful, a perfect picture of beautiful and majestic desolate-ness, drew all eyes and riveted the attention of all upon the grand scene.

I had never before realised that the Mountains of the Moon existed, assuming that, like Shangri-la, they had been thought up by someone disgruntled by the limitations of the known world. Someone who – like me – hoped there might be somewhere out there, strange, magical and undiscovered, and in the absence of any evidence had simply gone ahead and invented it.

That night I went round to Edward's flat. We were going to read each other passages from our novels and make critical comments on what we had written. I was prepared to do anything to get out of this. The potential for humiliation was almost limitless. I looked at my meagre bundle of material and wondered what to do. There were few options, the most viable of which seemed to be declaiming what I had written in a musical sing-song style suggested by hearing a record of Dame Edith Sitwell chanting the libretto to *Façade*. That, I felt, might at least alarm Edward sufficiently to deter any further inquiries.

He lived in a flat above a draper's shop off the Kingsland Road in Dalston. The bath was in the kitchen and in the yard outside hundreds of red telephones boxes were stacked together awaiting renovation by the Post Office. Edward was getting ready when I arrived. He was tugging at his beard, kneeling beside several thick piles of paper laid out on the living room carpet.

'What's that?' I asked, pointing to one of the piles.

'It's a sort of apocrypha,' said Edward.

This was even worse than I expected. There was nothing else for it now. I thought of Stanley marching at sunset, the mountains peeking out beside him. In Dalston the sun slid behind the massed ranks of telephone boxes. The sky darkened from grey to black. 'Have you ever heard of the Mountains of the Moon?' I asked.

Edward looked up in surprise. 'Of course,' he said. 'They're in Uganda.' He pulled out an atlas from the bookshelf. It had been printed in the 1920s. Most of Africa was still coloured red. Somewhere around the middle of East Africa there was a tiny brown smudge, speckled with flecks of white. It looked like an old bird dropping. Underneath was written Ruwenzori Mountains. After it, in brackets and smaller print, was written the Mountains of the Moon.

'There,' said Edward. 'That's them. Everyone used to think the Nile rose there. Mohammad believed that's where the Garden of Paradise was.'

'What are they like?'

'Very strange, apparently. It's one of the only places in the world where the phenomenon of gigantism can be observed.'

'Are you quoting from something?'

'I might be,' said Edward. 'I can't remember. Anyway, it's true. Things that grow 6 inches high everywhere else grow to about 20 feet in the Mountains of the Moon.'

'What sort of things?'

'Heather. They have whole forests of heather. And giant lobelias.'

I looked at the brown smudge and tried to remember if I knew what a normal sized lobelia looked like.

'Anyway,' said Edward, shutting the atlas, 'Do you want to start?'

I took out my bundle of paper. 'Chapter One' was written in pencil on the top sheet. My first sentence stared back up at me accusingly, like the victim of some linguistic attack. 'Turnips crunched beneath our hooves as we rode those last few miles to Lublin,' I began.

'Excuse me,' said Edward. 'Are you writing from the point of view of a horse?'

'No,' I said. 'At least, I don't think so.'

I composed myself once more. 'Turnips . . .'

'Wait,' said Edward. 'What's that?'

Up the stairwell came the sound, faint at first and then unmistakable, of sobbing. The sobbing grew steadily in volume. Great shuddering breaths rose from downstairs. I wondered if someone else had heard my first sentence and had fallen into understandable gloom. We went to investigate.

The only lavatory in the building was shared with the bedsit downstairs where Mr Adioga lived. He had come over from Nigeria to study land economy at North London Polytechnic, leaving his wife and two children behind. The course lasted two years, after which he would be able to go back to Nigeria and get a well-paid job.

Mr Adioga was quite unsuited to life in England. He couldn't take it at all. Even in summer he went about swathed in scarves and with sweaters bulging out the shoulders of his jacket. He hardly knew anyone and spent his evenings alone in his bedsit, studying and listening to the World Service. Occasionally he would come upstairs for some tea. He behaved like someone unused to human contact, seldom saying anything and sitting blowing the top of his mug long after he had drunk all his tea.

The door to Mr Adioga's bedsit was open. Music was playing. Mr Adioga was lying on his bed, crying uncontrollably, an empty bottle of port beside him. His cheeks shone with tears. 'What's the matter?' we asked. It took some time for Mr Adioga to calm down sufficiently to tell us.

'I've graduated,' he cried. 'Now I can go home. I'm so happy.'

From then on I discovered a new purpose to our visits to the Reading Room. I began to read about the Mountains of the Moon. It was like finding that my dreams had been plundered to create history. Edward was right. Mohammad had thought that the Garden of Paradise could be found there. But Mohammad was only one in a long line stretching from the Ancient Greeks to David T. Chantler – scriptwriter of the Hammer production of *She* – who had speculated at length, and often very excitedly, about the Mountains of the Moon. It was as if every theory about the mystery which lay at the heart of Africa had found a home there.

Most of these theories had to do with the source of the Nile. Around 1000 BC a contemporary of Homer had drawn a map of Africa on which the Nile was traced to an enormous range of mountains. Beyond the mountains nothing is marked, save one word: Pygmies. But in 1000 BC the map of Africa looked more like Crete, with Libya up at the top, Ethiopia to the east and west and nothing much underneath.

Five hundred years later Herodotus visited Egypt and travelled up the Nile as far as Elephantine. It's here that speculation really starts to take wing. Herodotus mentions having met a priest who told him, without a glimmer of uncertainty, that he knew just where the source of the Nile was.

The priest spoke of two mountains called Crophi and Mophi. In the centre of each mountain was an enormous fountain gushing forth vast streams of water. These joined up to become the Nile. The King of the region had tried to measure the depth of the fountains by letting down a very long rope into the mouth of each to see if it would touch the bottom. It hadn't, and the King concluded that the fountains were bottomless.

Herodotus, however, had his doubts about this. He smelled a rat: 'This was the priest's information on the truth of which I presume not to determine,' he noted in his journal.

None the less, the story stuck that the Nile rose from the earth in two enormous fountains. By Ptolemy's time (AD 90 to AD 168), the map of Africa had begun to fill out. Ptolemy was the first man to put the source of the Nile south of the Equator and the first to mention the Mountains of the Moon. He believed that the great fountains (or 'coy fountains', as they were to become known in deference to their elusiveness), were situated in the Mountains of the Moon, a range of mountains about 50 miles long, running east to west somewhere in the middle of Africa.

Just what prompted Ptolemy to christen them the Mountains of the Moon has never been properly explained. During the Dark Ages a number of Arabs had ventured deep into East Africa and there are several mentions in their accounts of the Mountains of Gumr. *Gumr* was believed to be a bastardisation of the word *Kama*, meaning moon. But it's just as likely that it's derived from the word *Kumr*, which means an object that's pale green in colour. Perhaps when faced with a choice between the Mountains of the Moon and the Mountains Resembling Objects that are Pale Green in Colour, Ptolemy took the romantic option and plumped for the former.

There is one more theory about the real meaning of the word *Gumr*. One of the early Arab travellers, Abu el Fadel, writing around

AD 1098 suggested that the mountains are so called, 'because the eye is dazzled by the great brightness'.

Abu el Fadel goes on to give one of the most intriguing accounts of what one might expect to find in the Mountains of the Moon:

> Some have said that certain people have reached these mountains and ascended there and looked over the other side where they saw a sea with troubled waters, dark as the night. This sea being traversed by a white stream, bright as the day which enters the mountains from the north, and passes by the grave of the Great Hermes, and Hermes is the prophet Idrisi.
>
> It is said that Idrisi there built a dome. Some say that people have ascended the mountains and one of them began to laugh and clap his hands and threw himself down the other side of the mountain. The others were afraid of being seized with the same fit and so came back. It is said that those who saw it saw bright snows like white silver gleaming with light. Whoever looked at them became attracted and stuck to them until they died and this science is called Human Magnetism.
>
> It is said that a certain king sent an expedition to discover the Nile sources and they reached copper mountains and when the sun rose the rays reflected were so strong they were burnt.
>
> It is said that in the days of Am Kaam, one of the kings of Egypt, Idrisi was taken up to heaven and he prophesied the coming of the flood so he remained on the other side of the Equator and there built a palace on the slopes of Mount Gumr. He built it out of copper and made 85 statues of copper, the waters of the Nile flowing through the mouths of these statues and then flowing into a great lake and thence to Egypt.

This was more like it. Troubled waters ... a dome ... a copper palace ... eighty-five copper statues ... Mount Gumr made Xanadu sound like a Territorial Army camp. It had been a long lay-off, but once again I began to have dreams about the Mountains of the Moon. It was like returning to familiar ground. There I was, back in buff fatigues (larger this time), splashing about in the great fountains and finally discovering the eighty-five statues from whose mouths the

31

Nile spewed forth. Occasionally – just to vary things – I would go walking in the Garden of Paradise, skirt Idrisi's Dome, and suffer a mild attack of Human Magnetism.

But it was clear that Abu el Fadel had had no more idea where the Mountains of the Moon were than I did. They were there all right. No one doubted this. But just where was to prove extraordinarily difficult to ascertain. Between Ptolemy's time and the mid-nineteenth century, the Mountains of the Moon bob around on different maps of Africa. One century they are south of the Equator, the next they have shifted back north again.

Julius Caesar and Alexander the Great sent expeditions up the Nile, but both were forced to turn back, overcome by heat, disease and hostile natives. Caesar is reputed to have said that he would abandon a battle to see 'the primal fountains of the Nile'.

Sebastian Cabot's map, drawn in the sixteenth century, has Africa more or less the right shape, with the Nile rising in what Cabot called the Mons Lune. Reproducing the map in his *In Darkest Africa*, Stanley noted sniffily, 'I have omitted the pictures of elephants and crocodiles, great emperors and dwarves which are freely scattered over the map with somewhat odd taste.' This is typical of Stanley – knock out anything superfluous, brush aside the fanciful.

Stanley was writing in 1896, almost forty-five years after Burton and Speke had had their famous falling-out over the source of the Nile, in which the Mountains of the Moon played a significant role. In 1853, while staying at Shepherd's Hotel in Cairo, Burton had heard a German missionary talking about the White Nile and the Mountains of the Moon. He had not been impressed. 'These stories,' he wrote, 'reminded me of a De Lunatico.' And indeed the notion that there could be a range of snow-capped peaks on the Equator had been widely ridiculed. Yet the stories fuelled Burton's growing obsession with finding the source of the Nile. The next year, he began planning an expedition from Somalia west to the Atlantic, believing that if he picked the right latitude he would have to hit the source sooner or later.

Burton anticipated bureaucratic difficulties in organising the expedition, particularly from the British army authorities in Aden.

'Our difficulties will be principally among that penis-cutting people,' he noted gloomily – Burton was not one to pass up any opportunity to refer to sexual mutilation.

In 1858, after numerous delays and revisions, Burton set forth, accompanied by his loyal companion John Hanning Speke. They sailed to Kaole, south of Zanzibar, and struck inland. The expedition was not a success. Almost everything that could go wrong did. They discovered Lake Tanganyika, but soon afterwards Burton fell ill. So did Speke. Burton's hearing at one point failed altogether and his eyesight deteriorated so badly that it was thought he was going blind. The two men rested up at the town of Kazeh, 500 miles east of Zanzibar.

Speke recovered more quickly than Burton and was keen to investigate reports of an even bigger lake than Lake Tanganyika, only sixteen days' march away. Burton was not at all taken with this idea. Relations between them had been deteriorating badly. Burton's ego had never before let him admit that Speke might be capable of independent thought, let alone locomotion. But now, still weak from disease, he had to lie back and watch as Speke set off northwards. By his own account he was delighted to see the back of him.

After exactly sixteen days' march Speke arrived at the shores of another great lake, apparently even larger than Lake Tanganyika. He took the elevation and found that the new lake also lay considerably higher. Standing on the shore, gazing out across an expanse of water that one of his porters believed 'probably extended to the end of the world', Speke was assailed by a blinding certainty. This was it, he had discovered the source of the Nile.

He named the lake Victoria and celebrated by shooting some red geese – a characteristic piece of self-expression from Speke, whose appetite for slaughtering wildlife almost matched that of Stanley. Three days later he set off again to tell Burton of his find. Burton was furious. He heaped scorn on Speke's claims, refusing even to listen to the reasons behind his assertion. The subject was taboo.

Burton simply could not accept that Speke might have got there first. He clung to the idea that the Nile rose, not in a lake, but in a range of mountains, with the Mountains of the Moon being the most likely candidates. Speke would have none of this. On his map he drew in the Mountains of the Moon between Lake Tanganyika and Lake Victoria. Burton countered by placing them between Lake Victoria and the most southerly known point of the Nile. In fact, Burton was closer to the truth. But this was a small victory. In his heart he knew that Speke had snatched the great prize from his grasp. He had lost the Nile.

It was not until thirty years later that the Mountains of the Moon were fixed on the map when on 26 April 1885 Stanley and his party came to the foothills of the Ruwenzori. Stanley had first set eyes on the Mountains of the Moon ten years earlier. From some distance away he had seen what he originally took to be a cloud mass, but then believed to be a number of snow-capped peaks. This time, though, he was sure. They set up camp in the foothills. 'Paths were seen leading up the steep slopes; a fine, cool river was 200 feet below rushing through the gorge fresh from the snow tops and of 61 degrees Fahrenheit temperature,' he noted. Stanley, however, was ill. He could barely walk 200 yards without assistance. Accordingly, he called for volunteers. 'I sounded the note to prepare to win immortal renown by scaling the heights of the famous Mountains of the Moon.' The response was not encouraging. Most of the party had also, like Stanley, come down with the fever. Everyone cried off, except Lieutenant W. G. Stairs who, 'taking a sly glance at the grim unconquered heights, said, "I'll go like a shot."'

Stairs departed with a party of forty Zanzibari porters on the morning of 6 June. They climbed through thick vegetation into the mist that shrouded the peaks. 'A general feeling of cold dampness prevailed,' he wrote. Several of the Zanzibaris, while 'remaining in good spirits' and intrigued by the idea of touching snow, complained of fever. The following morning he encountered the first of what appeared to be a series of ravines. Stairs realised that he had neither the provisions nor the food to cross the ravines and reluctantly turned back. He had reached a height of 10,677 feet and estimated that the highest peak in the range was about 17,000 feet. By three o'clock that afternoon he was back in camp with Stanley.

The terrain had not been particularly hazardous, he reported, although the mist was a constant problem. It was difficult to get any clear idea of what lay at the tops of the peaks. Even down at their camp in the foothills, the mist was apt to close in without warning. 'Thick, sluggish mist soared over the whole in irregular streams or in one heavy mass, which gave it the aspect of an inverted sky,' wrote Stanley. 'Sometimes for a brief period a faint image of endless woods loomed out, but the mist streamed upwards through the foliage as though a multitude of great geysers emitted vapours of steam.'

But now the Mountains of the Moon had been pinpointed, their latitude and longitude fixed. It seemed only a matter of time before they yielded up their secrets. Rider Haggard had finished *She* three years earlier in 1885, the same year that *King Solomon's Mines* had been published. One can imagine him, working against time, taking his imagination out for one last great fling, before lost civilisations were driven from the map, and Africa drawn and quartered beneath the cartographer's pencil.

Before long the rout was underway. But the Mountains of the Moon hung on to their power to set imaginations spinning for a while longer. In 1898 one S. Begge climbed up to a height of 9,000 feet. His servant climbed higher and came back with reports of finding a small lake on the shores of which were a number of black birds the size of sheep. When he tried to get close to them, they bellowed at him like bulls and he ran away. Far from thinking his servant mad, or affected with altitude sickness, Begge was only sad that he had not seen the black birds himself.

The real exploration work in the Ruwenzori was done in 1906 by the Italian explorer the Duke of Abruzzi. He led an expedition into the mountains for one of the most concerted bursts of climbing and mapping ever undertaken. In forty days he and his party climbed thirty peaks, and by the time they left there was little of the region left undiscovered. Of the eighty-five copper statues, the coy fountains, Idrisi's Dome and the huge black birds, they found no sign at all.

But even without these wonders visitors consistently reported being awestruck by the place. In 1934 the botanist Patrick Millington Synge went to the Mountains of the Moon to collect samples of

plant-life. He had little idea what to expect. What he found astonished him. He wrote:

A grey mist made a fitting background for the most monstrous
and unearthly landscape I have ever seen . . . Vague outlines of
peaks and precipices towered around us. Here were plants
which seemed more like ghosts of past ages than ordinary trees
and herbs. They appeared as a weird and terrible dream to me,
a botanist and hunter of strange plants. It all seemed unreal like
some imaginary reconstruction of life in a long past geographical
age, or even upon another planet. Our own familiar common
herbs seemed to have gone mad. We saw groundsels, swollen
and distorted, with woody trunks 20 feet in height, lobelias like
gigantic blue and green obelisks, heather mighty as giant trees.
Most alpine plants are reduced to extreme dwarfness, but these
have rushed to the opposite extreme and exhibit an exaggerated
gigantism. On the ground grew a thick carpet of mosses. Some
were brilliant yellow, others deep crimson in colour. Every shade
of green was represented. The tree trunks were also clothed in
thick moss, often tussocked into the semblance of faces, while
from their branches dangled long streamers of a pale sulphurous
yellow lichen, like old man's beard.

I did my best to share in Synge's 'weird and terrible dream'. When
I went to bed at night I would set myself a sleep agenda, a dream
itinerary, on which Synge was invariably head of the list. The mosses
erupted like goitres, the long sulphureous yellow lichen streamers
dangled down into my subconscious.

Immediately after my discovery of the Mountains of the Moon I
resolved to go there as soon as possible. It would be the fulfilment of
a childhood ambition. Not only that, but it would enrich my inner
life enormously. At last I would find something to write about.

And yet, at the same time I had my doubts. There was a lot to be
said for letting the Mountains of the Moon remain undisturbed, save
in my imagination. I thought of one of my childhood heroes, Sir
Francis Younghusband, who had dreamed for years of being the first
European to enter Lhasa, capital of Tibet. What would he find there?

The possibilities seemed endless. Both Herodotus and Ptolemy had also speculated about Tibet, wondering what might lie beyond the Himalayas. Here surely one would encounter the fantastic, the inexplicable, the fabulously exotic.

Younghusband had intended to try and make his way to Lhasa alone in 1889, when he was twenty-six, disguised as a Turki trader. But his commanding officer had refused him permission to go. Fifteen years later he got his chance, at the head of an army of more than 1,000 men. In attendance were more than 10,000 coolies and a small band of reporters including Edward Candler of the *Daily Mail*. At the beginning of August 1904 after a battle in which more than 700 Tibetans were killed, Younghusband and his army stood at the gates of Lhasa.

'Golden domes shone in the sun like tongues of fire,' wrote Candler in a state of great excitement. But once inside Lhasa, his enthusiasm rapidly subsided. This was not what they had expected at all. Expectations were cruelly dashed. The place was a tip. 'We found the city squalid and filthy beyond description, undrained and unpaved,' he wrote. 'Not a single house looked clean or cared for. The streets after rain are nothing but pools of stagnant water frequented by pigs and dogs searching for refuse.'

A trip to the Mountains of the Moon held the same dangers of disappointment. For a while, at least, there could be no question of going. In Uganda Idi Amin was in power. No one went anywhere near the place without a very good reason.

In Britain, Amin was still regarded as a figure of fun; dangerous certainly, but such a buffoon that he couldn't be taken too seriously. Thus the stories of persecution and torture that emerged from Uganda became diluted by ridicule and were largely ignored. In 1975 the then Foreign Secretary James Callaghan had been forced to go to Kampala to plead for the life of a British author detained there. But even this seemed to do more damage to Callaghan's reputation than to Amin's.

Meanwhile in Kampala terror gangs roamed the streets at night driving old Peugeots without number plates. They wore flared trousers, platform-soled shoes and dark glasses with thick perforated metal sides. You could be picked up on the slightest pretext. Detainees were interrogated, robbed, tortured and invariably killed.

The economy had collapsed. In the fifteen years since independence Uganda had gone from being one of the most prosperous countries in Africa to the verge of bankruptcy. Corruption was endemic, hospitals closed for lack of funds, people fled Kampala for their villages where they could lie low and grow enough food to survive. Just about the only Europeans who ventured there were aid workers trying to stop various projects from collapsing altogether.

Slowly – imperceptibly for a while – things began to get out of control. Edward and I both became journalists. Edward specialised in writing about East Africa. I was the cinema editor of a listings magazine, bought by first-time foreign visitors to London who didn't know any better.

Every week there was a large box on the inside front page of the magazine where an advertisement should have been – the only advertising revenue came from massage parlours and hostess bars, and even these were dropping off fast. It said, 'Remember to read our star columnists.' There followed four names, including my own, all of them quite unknown to any section of the reading public.

Most of my job consisted of compiling a list of the forthcoming programmes of cinemas around London. It was duller than I had ever imagined. There was a cinema in Tottenham that showed pornographic films and was run by a Pakistani man with a cleft palate. He would phone every Wednesday afternoon at four o'clock. I dreaded our conversations. They could go on for hours. 'Did you say Sexy Swedish Nymphets?' I would ask. There would be enraged cries from the other end of the phone. 'Saucy Susan Strips Off?' More shouts of protest. 'Sizzling Secrets of Surburbia?'

One Wednesday just before four o'clock the phone rang. Indistinct tones came down the line. They sounded more like vowels than consonants. 'Are You Getting Enough?' I hazarded.

'It's me,' whispered Edward. 'I can't talk for long. I'm flying to Kampala tonight.'

It was October 1983. In Uganda, Amin had been toppled four

years earlier and the previous President, Milton Obote, restored to power. But any hopes that the new government would signal a return to stability had soon disappeared. Obote's first period in office, following independence in 1961, had been relatively peaceful. The economy was stable, the standard of living improved. Obote was not about to make the same mistake twice. This time he simply carried on where Amin had left off. The killings, the torturings, the economic chaos continued unchecked.

After the rigged elections of February 1981 which returned Obote to power, one of his former army commanders Yoweri Museveni went into the bush to form a guerrilla force called the National Resistance Army. Consisting at first of just twenty-six soldiers, Museveni's forces had swollen rapidly. Campaigning on a slogan of 'Clean Leadership and Unity', they pledged to restore order, unite the various warring tribal factions and root out corruption.

Throughout Obote's second regime rumours filtered out of Uganda of atrocities carried out by government troops. But there was little or no first hand evidence. No western journalist had been allowed into the areas where massacres were believed to have taken place.

Two nights after Edward arrived in Kampala he and an NRA representative slipped through the Kampala curfew and in the next two and half days walked the 100 miles to the guerrilla lines.

He spent two weeks with Museveni's troops, collecting evidence of massacres. In Luwero Province alone 25,000 people are estimated to have been killed between 1981 and 1985.

In January 1986 the NRA advanced into Kampala. They fought a pitched battle on the golf course near the centre of the city, advancing up the fairways and taking cover in the bunkers. When the Obote soldiers realised they were losing, they threw off their army uniforms and started running away. But even their red underpants were army issue. Torn between modesty and self-preservation, a number were shot with their underpants hitched around their knees. For days afterwards the golf course was strewn with bodies. Residents at the nearby Fairway Hotel who liked to take their meals on the balcony, and had continued to do so throughout the fighting, complained that the smell of decomposing bodies was spoiling their appetites.

Museveni was sworn in as President. Soon afterwards Edward was asked to come out to Kampala and edit a new national newspaper. By now wheels were in motion – had already advanced some way, although I was only just beginning to realise it. I felt as if I was on automatic pilot, being borne along to a predetermined destination – without protest, but without much in the way of volition either.

When Edward came back to England we discussed going to the Mountains of the Moon. It was not the first time we had discussed such a trip. But the air of bogus practicality we normally adopted on such occasions had been replaced by something quite different.

'Gaiters,' said Edward. 'We must have gaiters.'

'What are they?'

'Things to stop water getting into your boots.'

We would have to have porters of course, and a guide. Food and equipment would have to be airfreighted out in advance. Edward was flying back to Kampala. I would join him out there in a month's time. I made notes, watching my hand move back and forth across the page, wondering how it could possibly have come to this.

At a shop in an underpass below the Strand I bought a giant tub of something called Joe Weider's Dynamic Carbo-energiser. It was on the shelf next to various steroid solutions and appetite suppressants. In the dim light of the shop, bulky figures moved around touching the plastic drums like sacred vessels. I looked about in a state of acute self-consciousness. Everyone else was twice my width. The shop assistant had bumps under his shirt that bore no relation to any known anatomical model. I told him that I wanted something that would compensate for my lack of fitness and keep me in a constant state of hyperactivity. He reached unerringly for Joe Weider's Dynamic Carbo-Energiser. There was a picture of Joe Weider on the front. Whatever else his Dynamic Carbo-Energiser had done for him, it had certainly done wonders for his pigmentation. His face was a furious tangerine colour with a faint phosphorescent glow round his hairline. I stared at the picture of Joe and wondered if he had any idea just how much faith I was investing in him.

40

Edward had asked me to bring out two books for an Intelligence officer in the Ugandan Secret Service. One was Peter Wright's *Spycatcher*. The other was about the CIA's activities in Africa. No one was quite sure of the title, although the Intelligence officer thought it might be called *Hunting Down Your Enemies*. As titles go this had a lot going for it; snappy, forceful, free from any risk of misinterpretation. In every bookshop I tried the assistants stared at me with incredulity that gave way to alarm when they realised I was serious. No one admitted to having heard of it. After a while I decided to abandon the search and pride myself instead on having the sort of conscience that knows just where to draw the line.

On the plane from Nairobi to Entebbe a priest in a frayed dog-collar snored softly in the seat beside me. I opened my copy of *She* and read once again the opening paragraph:

In giving to the world the record of what, considered as an adventure only, is, I suppose, one of the most wonderful and mysterious experiences ever undergone by mortal men, I feel it incumbent on me to explain my exact connexion with it. So I will say at once that I am not the narrator but only the editor of this extraordinary history, and then go on to tell how it found its way into my hands.

There was thick cloud outside. The plane swept low over Lake Victoria towards Entebbe Airport. In the next seat, the priest stirred, awoke momentarily, looked out of the window and went back to sleep. A number of other priests were on the plane, all showing signs of wear and stretched out asleep in the aisle seats. The stewardess had to step across a tangle of clerical legs as she went back to her seat to strap herself in for landing. All at once the plane broke through the cloud and there in front was a hill covered with the greenest vegetation I had ever seen. It was a bright luminous green that stared up angrily from the ground, defying us to land.

The plane circled the runway and then made its approach. The priest beside me woke up and began intoning something to himself, his lips moving animatedly enough but producing only a low, faintly remonstrative sounding mumble. We touched down and taxied over to the terminal, a square grey building with a line of people along the roof, shielding their eyes from the sun. I looked for Edward, but it was impossible to make anyone out.

Everyone began collecting their baggage from the lockers. I was one of the last to leave, staring at my copy of *She* and then at the view through the porthole. It didn't look like the same sort of place at all.

Outside the smell of aircraft fuel was overpowering. You could hardly breathe. Several of the passengers pulled their coats over their faces and broke into a run, hesitantly at first, then picking up speed as they hurried away from the plane and sprinted for the open doors of the terminal.

Four

Three hundred yards outside Entebbe Airport there is an army roadblock. The thinking here is straightforward enough. Customs officials at the airport have long been notorious for demanding bribes. At one point things got so bad that even Ugandan politicians returning from abroad had to shell out to get back into their own country. But while the customs were diligent in their collection of backhanders, they were nothing compared to the army, who threw themselves into the task with an awesome kind of gusto.

Things, though, had changed. The old army had been routed and a new one had taken its place, one that prided itself on having weeded out corrupt elements. The customs, however, had still not quite managed to slough off all their old habits. They needed watching. Hence the roadblock to trap the unwary. Passengers who had taken all the usual steps to ease their passage through customs now found the real hurdle waiting just down the road.

Four men in combat fatigues waved us on to the verge. They had machine guns slung round their shoulders, shirts open to the waist and short green gumboots on their feet. We stopped beside a large wooden arch. Two carved birds bent towards one another either side of the tarmac, their beaks touching above the centre of the road. Picking at a pile of rubbish nearby were a group of Marabou storks. They were enormous, the size of beefy children hitting their teens. Their black feathers were stiff with dirt. Under their throats food pouches, red and distended, shuddered about as they walked.

'I hate those bloody birds,' said Edward.

One of the soldiers stared at me for a few moments and then told me to get out of the pick-up and open my luggage. I pulled out bundles of clothes, unrolling them for him to see. He jerked his gun barrel at the washbag down at the bottom of my case. I unzipped it and he peered inside. My face flannel was wrapped around two packets of Durex. He jerked the gun barrel again. As I unwrapped the bundle I thought that it comprised one of the most pitiful sights I had ever seen, a sad little tableau beaming out all sorts of reproachful messages about the folly of sexual desire.

The soldier couldn't have been more than sixteen. He picked up one of the packets, shook it and stared at me again. I grinned in a loose, apologetic sort of way, like someone beset by terrible foibles he cannot hope to understand. One of the other soldiers came over and picked up the other packet. For a while the two of them rattled my Durex around like maracas. Then the first soldier smiled and said, 'It is good to love carefully.'

'It is?'

'Oh yes,' he said. 'You must remember.'

The two soldiers handed me back the packets of Durex. I crammed them back into my washbag and got into the pick-up.

'What was all that about?' asked Edward.

'He told me that I should be careful in my lovemaking.'

'So you should,' said Edward. 'Especially here.'

'Love More Carefully' turned out to be one of the government anti-AIDS slogans. It had been chosen to spearhead the government's AIDS awareness campaign, along with the less direct but infinitely more touching 'Beware the Sweetness and Splendour of Sex'. Uganda, along with its neighbour Ruanda, was already one of the world's AIDS blackspots. Recent tests had shown that over 20 per cent of sexually active adults in Kampala were HIV positive. But the government's campaign had been widely criticised for not being hard-hitting enough and was thought to be having little effect.

We drove along the narrow road that ran round the shores of Lake Victoria, Speke's great sea that extended to the end of the world. Far out from the shore you could see light flecks on the water where the wind whipped up white horses. On the other side of the road, covered in a tangle of vegetation and speckled with rust, was the remains of an aircraft, the plane the Israelis had stormed in their famous raid on Entebbe in 1975. The airport had since been moved, but the plane had remained, slewed into a bank and left to rot.

Half a mile further on there was another roadblock. Here again the principle was simple. It's possible that you may have squeezed through both the customs and the first road block – no one claims total incorruptibility for the army. By now you'd probably be feeling pretty pleased with yourself. Two obstacles safely negotiated and a clear run to Kampala in prospect. And then, up ahead, something quite new in the miscreant control line – a second roadblock.

We were waved over to the verge again. There were more soldiers here. They looked even younger than the ones back down the road. Several had taken off their green gumboots and were lying on the grass. The boots were laid out in two rows in front of them. A couple of soldiers were urinating against a tree. They finished and wandered over to the pick-up. This, Edward told me, had been one of the most notorious killing grounds during the Amin years. Few travellers showing any signs of prosperity made it past the Amin soldiers, especially at night when they tended to be drunk and more trigger-happy than usual. People were dragged from their cars, robbed, beaten up and often shot. Bodies were dumped in the shallows where willows now overhung clumps of bullrushes. At one point so many bodies were thrown into Lake Victoria that they blocked the pipes carrying the main water supply to Kampala. Even now fishermen still found their lines getting snagged around corpses.

One of the soldiers took my passport, his gaze switching back and forth between my face and my passport photo. 'Her Majesty's Secretary of State Requests and Requires . . .' He stopped and laughed in a thin, high-pitched voice. It wasn't a particularly threatening or unpleasant laugh, but it still made my insides writhe around in fright. The discovery of my Durex had made me even more jittery than usual. That and all these sustained bouts of scrutiny. Being on the receiving end of anything more direct than the most hurriedly averted glance had always induced hot flushes of shame. Of course, the fact that there was no apparent reason to feel ashamed only made it worse. You may have forgotten your own guilty secret. That was immaterial. Nobody else had.

There was something watery about the soldier's eyes, more conjunctival than grief-stricken. Little crystals of sleepy-dust trailed down his nose. He blinked hard, handed me back my passport and waved us on with a dismissive flick of his hand.

A boy on a bicycle weaved about on the road in front of us. A large fish was draped over the back wheel, its tail fin brushing the spokes. 'Nile perch,' said Edward. 'The British threw some in the lake as an experiment and they grew to four times their normal size.'

As surreptitiously as possible I took out my notebook. The road surface was so uneven that writing was almost impossible, but still I managed to scrawl, 'Boy on Bike. Fish on Back,' on the front page.

'What are you doing?' said Edward.

'I'm taking notes.'

'Whatever for?'

'I thought I might try and write a book.'

'What sort of book?'

The pick-up hit a bump and leapt into the air. The boy on the bicycle veered off the road towards the trees, struggling to stay upright. His fish bucked on the back wheel as if it was still alive.

'Something about our trip.'

It was almost eight years since our daily trips to the British Museum had petered out. Since then things had not improved. Indeed, they'd got to the point where I used to look back wistfully to the bouts of sustained creativity I had enjoyed in the Museum Reading Room. The chances of my ever getting between covers – hard, soft, even cardboard, I wasn't fussy – looked to have receded for good. For journalists especially, books are a touchy subject. Most journalists aspire to writing one, few traditionally make it. Those who do have to put up with glowering resentment from those who haven't. And no wonder. Writing a book was a way of elevating yourself above the realms of the ephemeral – where other journalists remained stuck – and putting some sort of claim on posterity. Naturally everyone hated you for it.

That was bad enough, but what made it worse was the fact that just about everybody I knew had written books. Normally, those who still dreamed of literary careers could seek one another out for a bit of solace, a trip round the shops to see whose latest effort had just been remaindered. But I seemed to be the only one left. Functional illiterates, people with rampaging forms of dyslexia, even those who claimed to have no interest at all in writing had made it into print. You'd see them at parties and ask them with an increasing sense of foreboding what they were up to. 'I'm writing a book,' they'd say. They spoke of it bashfully, as if confessing to awkward impulses they had no control over. And every time I'd fall into the same trap, unable to choke back the indignant retort. 'Another one? But you've only just finished the last one.' Then they'd shrug apologetically and move away to join someone else equally bent low under the stigma of publication.

'A book about me?' said Edward.

'And me. I'd be in it too.'

'A travel book?'

'That sort of thing.'

'A big book?'

'I wouldn't have thought so.'

'Are you going to put in bits about your childhood?'

'I don't know,' I said 'I might. Do you thing it's a good idea?'

'No,' said Edward. 'I do not. The whole thing sounds like utter self-indulgence. I hate books like that. They're all the same. The same old crap about trying to fulfil childhood fantasies. Awful. I thought you'd learned your lesson with all that stuff about the horse and the beetroot.'

'Turnips,' I said unhappily.

'Have you written anything recently?' he asked.

'No.' I said. 'Not recently.' This wasn't entirely true. For some months I had been toying with something big. Perhaps the biggest novel ever set on the Great Barrier Reef, but it hadn't quite worked out as I had hoped and there seemed little point in bringing it up.

'I suppose I can't stop you, but you can't carry on taking notes. It'll drive me mad. You'll just have to try and remember things.'

I tucked my notebook away into my bag. The road rose and fell towards Kampala over narrow ridges of hills. The greenery was even brighter on the ground than it had been from the air. There were several women walking along the side of the road in single file. They wore long cotton dresses with flounced sleeves and had bunches of green bananas on their heads. Piles of fruit and vegetables were laid out on trestle-tables. No one seemed to be buying any. I tried to fix things in my mind as we drove past. 'Women with green bananas,' I repeated to myself. 'Piles of papayas.' But as soon as I was sure I'd got one thing fixed, along came something else and chased it out again. It was like trying to build a house and finding that someone keeps stealing the foundations.

A train pulled its way up a long incline towards the railway station. Clouds of dark smoke shot out of the exhaust vents as the pistons faltered and then started churning again. Most of the passenger carriages had fallen to pieces years ago. Now people rode to work in cattle trucks. Some sat on the roof, others clung to the sides. Through the open doors ranks of commuters stood holding brief-cases. Up front men frantically gunned the motor for more power. The rails sagged and twanged as they took the weight – a deep, booming sound that heralded the approach of the train to passengers waiting down the line.

Men with oxyacetylene torches were welding bedsteads together by the side of the road. There was a stall selling coffins and a little further on another stall specialising in children's coffins. They were stacked up in piles 10 feet high, the smallest little bigger than shoe-boxes.

Towards the centre of Kampala the potholes grew steadily deeper and more cavernous. Here, said Edward, only the drunks drove in straight lines. Everyone else did a kind of crawling slalom round the craters. By contrast with the surrounding countryside the colour seemed to have drained out of Kampala. The place looked exhausted, almost monochrome. Everything was covered in pink dust, the houses, the cars, even the people. None of the buildings had been painted in years. Several of them still bore the scars of recent fighting – pediments shot away, walls peppered with bullet-holes and black-ened with scorch-marks.

Large office blocks started fifteen, even twenty years earlier and never completed, stood derelict in the centre of town, occasionally shedding chunks of masonry on passers-by. The mosque that Idi

48

Amin had built to mark the country's overnight conversion from Christianity to Islam in 1972 had never been completed either. It leaned heavily to one side, shrouded in scaffolding. The scaffolding had been there for so long that it too had begun to topple over towards the houses below. The whole thing stuck up like a broken limb that had been set without anyone bothering to straighten it first.

There was only one set of working traffic lights in Kampala. Few people took much notice of them. Every junction was a battleground with little wars of nerves being fought out among the drivers. You'd see them, revving their cars until the engines were screaming, waiting for a break in the traffic, trying to scare off the competition. One day later, I had lunch with a man who had been invited by the government to compile a census of all traffic accidents in Kampala over the last twelve months. The work was tough. It was really getting him down. He'd already had to move out of one office, evicted by mounting paperwork. Then there was the ridicule, people would howl with laughter whenever he told them what he was doing. Now he was close to breaking point. His girlfriend had told of how he had started babbling random statistics in his sleep. He was very smartly dressed in blazer and tie, but as he talked, sweat marks emerged from beneath his jacket and advanced across his chest. 'I just don't know how much longer I can stand this,' he kept saying.

Up on Kololo Hill were the great colonial bungalows built in the 1920s and 1930s, when Uganda was considered to be a more desirable and prestigious diplomatic posting than Nairobi, or anywhere else in East Africa. There too were vast Art Deco palaces stepped with balconies and verandas put up in the 1950s and 1960s by Asians who were subsequently expelled by Amin. Now their shutters hung loose, plasterwork crumbled, the balconies were unsafe, swimming pools stood empty and bulging as the pool walls were pressed towards one another. Creepers ran riot over the windows, moss erupted from between paving stones, paintwork blistered. You could have reshot *Sunset Boulevard* in any of them. Once there would have been any number of Norma Desmonds here, grand colonial hostesses chauffered around in cars lined with leopard skin. But that was an age ago.

By the market a man with no legs was lying on what was left of the pavement. On the other side of the road, separated by a particularly gargantuan pothole, a number of men were teasing him. They chucked pieces of bread at him and waggled their legs around to show what he was missing out on. The man was getting steadily more incensed. He raised himself up on his elbows and made as if to scuttle towards his tormentors. They were wheezing with laughter, literally creased up and slapping their hands on their knees. In Kampala, it rather looked as if you took your amusements wherever you could find them.

These were getting fewer all the time. Because of the AIDS crisis, business had dropped off badly among the bar-girls. The number of adults in Kampala who were HIV positive was climbing steadily. In the city's main hospital, deaths from AIDS among children under five had doubled in the last two years.

In the James Bond 007 Club, once a favourite haunt of Amin's henchmen, and now a home from home for all sorts of Kampala low-lifers, the mood was grim, the atmosphere one of perpetually thwarted expectation. To make matters worse there was a beer crisis. Supplies had been low for weeks and were rumoured to be on the verge of running out altogether. A group of prostitutes stood at one end of the bar casting resentful glances at the men who stood in a huddle at the other swigging bottles of fizzy orange. Recently it had been reported that in one town in Western Uganda things had got so bad that the women had started gang-raping men who no longer wished to avail themselves of their services. This was a favourite conversation piece in Kampala, especially among western men. Something to be discussed gravely and maturely, with only the faintest tremble of excitement. Meanwhile they practised a kind of sexual apartheid. Until the AIDS crisis it was quite usual for white men to have Ugandan girlfriends or mistresses. Not any longer. Now they stuck to their own. And white women who had had affairs with Ugandans now found themselves off-limits to white suitors.

On top of all the highest buildings Marabou storks stood in line, keeping watch on the city below. From the ground they looked like enormous vultures poised for action. At dusk they would fly down and scavenge for food, beating the air aside with huge black tattered wings.

Due to thefts of transformer oil from the electricity turbines parts of Kampala were periodically plunged into darkness. Ugandans had learned to live with an erratic power supply. The fridge in the main morgue had been out of action for years. Bags of ice normally used to keep drinks cool were brought in to delay decomposition. Bodies lay half submerged in melted ice while embalmers worked round the clock. Stealing was widespread. Most shopkeepers tried to take as much of their stock home with them as possible each evening, for fear that it would disappear during the night.

Just about the only thing booming in Kampala was religion. Ugandans just couldn't get enough of it. At least, the full range of Christian disciplines was being unrolled for them to take their pick. When the last war had eased up every conceivable kind of holy-roller had pitched into Uganda. (You had to be careful discussing wars in Uganda. Pinpointing just which one you were referring to could be difficult.) What pickings there were, what souls crying out for salvation. An entire population, poor, war-weary and desperate for any comfort going.

All around Kampala, there were posters bearing the slogan, 'See How God Loves Kampala.' To begin with I assumed that someone with a finely developed sense of irony had been hard at work here – it sounded just as redundant as Churchill's oft-quoted remark that Uganda was the pearl of Africa. But no, everyone took it very seriously. The only trouble was that the posters seemed to be stuck up on the most ruined, burnt-out and structurally perilous buildings. The message, to unbelievers anyway, seemed clear. Assuming God existed, there was no evidence whatsoever that Kampala figured anywhere in his plans.

On all the roads leading into the city, corrugated iron huts with little pitched roofs like cricket pavilions housed the various evangelist missions. In the space of 100 yards you could find Adventists (Sixth Day, Seventh Day, any millenarian catered for), fundamentalists, neo-fundamentalists, Mormons, Christian Scientists, even Plymouth Brethren.

With such a concentration of God's emissaries in one place, a certain amount of competitiveness had crept in. People were confused. They didn't know which evangelists to go for. Something more than guidance was called for. They needed encouragement. They needed Special Offers.

Stretched out across one of the roundabouts in the middle of town was a banner with 'Expect Miracles' written on it in red letters. Underneath it said, 'The Blind Will See, The Deaf Will Hear, The Lame Will Walk'. Next to it was a notice announcing the imminent arrival of the famous Australian evangelists, Cliff and Helen Beard. A huge marquee was being erected on the Entebbe road where Cliff and Helen would address the faithful and the curious.

The chances were that they would already have been softened up by regular television exposure to the American evangelist Jimmy Swaggart, who appeared every evening on Ugandan television. It wasn't long since Swaggart had been disgraced in America and his programmes taken off the air as the result of a sex scandal. There were no such problems in Uganda. For a start it was reckoned that Ugandans would probably take a more lenient view of any sexual misbehaviour than the Americans had done. And besides, his programmes were provided free of charge and the state television channel had no intention of letting them go to waste.

In one sense at least Swaggart was one of the more upright television regulars in Uganda. Presenters on home-grown programmes were hampered by the deficiencies of their equipment, particularly their camera tripods which all seemed to be missing legs. As a result, presenters tilted alarmingly to one side when they appeared on screen. This was apt to play havoc with viewers' sense of balance, especially if they were drunk. You'd see them in bars trying to line themselves up with the image on the television, at a complete loss to work out what the hell was going on.

While the majority of visiting evangelists now promised miracles – the thinking presumably being that they would be out of the country long before any backlash gathered force among those who had remained infirm – others had resorted to less direct ways of getting their message across. A few months earlier a new butcher's shop had opened in Kampala selling particularly delicious sausages. The quality of the sausages far outstripped that of any other sausages on offer elsewhere, and the butcher's quickly became very popular. After a while customers began to find little printed homilies wrapped up with their sausages. They spoke of the nature of life – bad alas, but with vast room for improvement – and the necessity of picking a safe path through the minefield with God's eternal hand to clutch on to. Later it emerged that the butcher's was owned by the Moonies. The news caused a slight falling-off in the sale of sausages, but the Moonies were undeterred. They were so delighted with the scheme that they were believed to be planning further sausage-led crusades elsewhere in the country.

But then this was simply a variation on a well accepted business principle in Uganda – that the combination of a dog-collar and some entrepreneurial flair was a surefire winner. The Archbishop of Kampala was a notable exponent of this theory, having set up and managed a successful provincial bus network, called – with a sly reference to the promise of one really big journey up ahead – the Gateway Bus Company.

Even Ugandan pop singers were not immune from religious fervour. Uganda is not renowned for its pop music. Every other country in the world may have had its ethnic music plundered by western record producers intent on uncovering the latest thing, but no one has come anywhere near Uganda. None the less the country has a few popular groups and singers. The pattern, though, is always the same. They make a few records, get a reputation for themselves, and are then struck down with a mysterious desire to turn into Jim Reeves. Presumably this has something to do with the number of American evangelists who have passed through, dispensing records of Country and Western crooners extolling their faith in song. The change is dramatic – no one is exempt. Singers who had hitherto disdained western influences suddenly don plaid shirts, learn the pedal steel guitar and start singing Reeves-type songs about 'Riding the Big Dipper to Salvation'.

Anyone doubting the turbulence of Uganda's recent past need only buy a street map of Kampala. Not that you'll be able to. None has been printed in years and those that are still around bear names that have been changed several times in the last few years. Edward lived on Baskerville Drive, a name comfortingly redolent of all things English – tweedy respectability threatened only by the occasional mad hound. But such colonial leftovers are increasingly rare; 50 yards outside the front gate Baskerville Drive ran into Malcolm X Avenue.

We pulled off the road and bounced along a rutted, unmetalled track. On the right behind clumps of bushes were fields of maize. This, said Edward, was a spot known locally as Castration Corner. Only the week before a group of witches had finally been caught after staging a number of nocturnal kidnappings. Victims had been dragged into the bushes where various voodoo rituals were enacted. A teenage girl had been disembowelled, a boy had had his testicles cut off, and an elderly man had somehow survived after being castrated and having slits cut in his cheeks in an attempt to remove his tongue.

Much to the despair of the government – and the evangelists, who took it as a personal slight – witchcraft had been staging something of a comeback in Uganda. The most serious threat to the new regime during their two years in power had come from a voodoo priestess called Alice Lakwena, who had amassed an army of 20,000 supporters. They had few guns or weapons but this, insisted Lakwena, was no drawback at all. She convinced her followers that if they anointed themselves with a special magic oil they would become invulnerable to bullets. Not only that, but rocks they threw would explode like grenades. Not altogether surprisingly, they suffered very heavy casualties in their first clash with government troops. Still, there were enough left alive to continue the campaign and new recruits swarmed in to replace the casualties. It was only after a further series of battles with even heavier losses that Lakwena and her supporters fled in disarray.

We pulled up outside two high metal gates, chained and padlocked. Edward banged on the horn. There was no sign of any movement

54

inside. We got out of the pick-up and waited for the houseboy to come and unlock the gates. It was getting dark. I looked at the bunches of red blossom that hung from the trees and stood out bright in the gathering gloom. And then I looked more closely at the gate. A line of bullet-holes ran across one of the gates in a kind of wave pattern.

'Edward,' I said. 'These bullet-holes . . . they look fresh.'

'Ugandans are really nice people,' he said. 'It's just they don't seem able to stop killing each other.'

'Each other is one thing. But what about this?'

'I've got a lot of enemies,' he said. He sounded rather apologetic. The houseboy jogged down the drive, dressed in shiny blue boxer shorts and carrying a bunch of keys.

I climbed back into the pick-up. It was one of those moments that called for some rapid rethinking, a hurried overhaul of priorities to take account of vital new information. Such as the fact that the person you've just travelled 2,000 miles to visit is an assassination target.

That night, lying in bed, I felt more lonely than I had done in years. The feeling came over me quite suddenly. It was like driving into a poison cloud. As a child I suffered from homesickness. This, however, doesn't begin to describe the scale of the problem. I was without any even remotely serious rivals in the field. The merest hint of separation from my parents had been enough to provoke torrents of grief. At Victoria Station it was not unusual to see small boys sniffling unhappily as they waited to catch one of the school trains down to the South Coast, quite deaf to the embarrassed entreaties of their parents. But they all shut up when they saw me coming. They knew they couldn't compete. Growing up, I waited impatiently for the time when I could venture off on my own without being overcome, first by panic and then by a kind of strangulated anguish.

It never came. If anything things got worse rather than better, mainly because they had slipped way past the point of rational explanation. Now there was no longer anything to feel homesick about. I didn't miss my parents. I didn't miss anything I could think of. But still, almost any sort of displacement played havoc with my defences.

This had all sorts of worrying implications. I pulled the sheet up to my neck and remembered how as a child bed had often seemed like the only refuge in a cold, unkind world. At school when I was eight or nine I slept next to a boy called Adams who wet his bed. This wasn't something that happened once in a while. Adams wet his bed every single night, without fail. Each morning there was a bed inspection. We had to pull back our blankets so that both top and bottom sheets could be scrutinised by the matron for anything untoward. She went at this with all the thoroughness of a forensic scientist, kneeling down and peering at each sheet as if she expected to find tiny incriminating particles stuck to the cotton.

However, no close inspection was required in Adams's case. Every morning he pulled back his blankets to reveal a large damp patch. I used to watch Adams's face carefully as the matron moved down the line towards his bed. He must have known what was coming, but his face never registered anything at all. He didn't tremble, swallow hard or turn pale. With an air of weariness and unconcealed distaste the matron would tell him to strip his bed and hang the offending sheet over his bedside chair to dry. It stayed there throughout the day, a flag of shame growing steadily yellower as the stain dried.

To begin with Adams was teased about this. He had few, if any, friends. Anyone who might have thought of striking up a friendship with him was put off by his reputation. But after a while it became clear that there was something terrible in his bedwetting. We all came to dread the morning inspection and would look away in embarrassment as he pulled back his bedclothes. He had been given a rubber undersheet long before, but this made no difference. It simply stopped the mattress from rotting and ensured that he lay steeped in his own urine.

I felt a strange sort of kinship with Adams. I wasn't his friend of course. But just as I was apt to burst into tears without warning, so he had no control over his bladder. We were united in incontinence. Then one day something extraordinary happened. The bed inspection was proceeding normally, the matron making her way towards

56

Adams's bed. As usual his face was quite expressionless. The matron told him to strip his bed. He pulled back the blankets. A ripple of surprise ran through the dormitory. There was nothing there. People inched forward to get a closer look. His bottom sheet was quite dry. The matron didn't believe it. You could tell she felt cheated. She even crouched down and looked under the bed in case he'd peed there instead, but there was nothing.

While no one said anything afterwards, there was a general sense of relief that Adams's stigma had been lifted. The mood on the following day's inspection was perceptibly lighter than usual. The matron came to Adams's bed. She smiled at him in an encouraging sort of way. He pulled back his bedclothes. The stain was back, bigger than ever as if to compensate for its day away. There was scarcely a dry patch left on the sheet. I remember how it clung to his bedside chair as Adams tried to drape it across to dry. And still his face registered nothing, at least nothing I could detect.

That night as I lay awake, carefully clenching my penile sphincter before allowing myself the luxury of sleep, I heard odd noises coming from Adams's bed. At first I thought it was the pipes – they were mounted on the walls and would gurgle and hiss throughout the night. Then I realised that Adams had his face buried in his pillow and was crying. I lay there wondering what to do. It seemed such a little thing to lean over and offer some words of comfort. After all, I did have some idea of what he was going through. And yet, I did nothing. Several times I was about to, but each time I thought, no, don't bother. I have to save my compassion for myself – there's none to spare.

The following term there was no sign of Adams. His parents had taken him away. No one bothered to say where he had gone and, as far as I knew, no one bothered to ask.

Five

It was Saturday. We would have to wait another four days before setting off for the mountains. There were more provisions to buy, transport to be sorted out. All of this was likely to prove time-consuming. Besides, nothing would happen until Monday. Things changed in Kampala at the weekends. Not just offices closing and people going away. Smaller, less obvious things.

On Saturdays the Sardinia Restaurant changed its menu from Italian to Chinese food. Just why was a mystery. The owner of the restaurant wasn't Chinese, nor was the chef. There were few Chinese people in Kampala apart from the embassy staff, and they seldom ate out. It was not even as if the restaurant was particularly popular on a Saturday due to the change of cuisine. Still, the pattern was set and no one saw any reason to mess with tradition.

At the bar several men were sitting on high metal stools. As soon as Edward and I walked in one of them, dressed in combat fatigues, got off his stool with some difficulty and stumbled towards us. 'Oh no,' muttered Edward. 'This could be awkward.' Two months earlier the man, who was one of the army commanders, had caused a huge fuss when he referred to anti-government rebels as 'biological substances.' This was held to be wildly intemperate language. The government had been embarrassed, the evangelists had hit the roof. It was quite disgraceful, they said, that a government official should refer to human beings in such derogatory terms. And then, of course, there was the whole theological issue of whether human beings were in fact biological substances at all, or creatures of quite a different order. Most of the evangelist groups had no truck at all with Darwinism, preaching instead that it still all came down to the snake in the grass, the apple and Adam's weak will.

The man had been severely reprimanded. Such language would not be tolerated, he was told. But he was rumoured to be quite unrepentant, even boastful. And now he was also very drunk. His index finger wavered about for a while and then pointed at my chest. I knew it would. In the few seconds before his finger came to rest, I was in no doubt at all which one of us he would pick on. Drunks, maniacs, the chronically disturbed sought me out with the unerring instinct of homing pigeons. In London it happened all the time. It was like some terrible kind of magnetism. On the street, in super-markets, lifts, anywhere remotely public, I could see them – the unsteady and unstable – finetuning their mental radar and bearing down on me.

On the Tube of course you were especially vulnerable. When I first arrived in London I had leaped to my feet at the first sign of infirmity. What a mistake this was. You had to put up with the murderous glances of fellow passengers who sat fast, immune to such crass forms of blackmail. And after a while, like everyone else, I stopped. Now pregnant women went into labour strap-hanging above me, while blind men tapped their way unaided into the path of oncoming trains.

But there was a price to be paid for all this. Everyone else got away with it, but not me. It was as if the price for disregarding other people's physical disabilities was that you got saddled with their mental ones instead. I lost count of the times I looked up to see someone thrusting things into my lap, tearing off pieces of their clothing, wailing and dancing frenzied jigs.

Not long before I had left London, a woman in her thirties – no obvious signs of lunacy – had sat beside me on the Tube. It was the beginning of the rush-hour and the carriages were starting to fill up. She reached into her bag, pulled out a pile of letters and began reading extracts from them. They were full of the most intimate details, interspersed with asides to me on the perfidy of men. I shrank towards the window beaming out mental disclaimers at the other passengers. She's Nothing To Do With Me. Nothing At All. The asides, which had started out as little explanatory fillers, became steadily more impassioned and then – as I knew they would – turned nasty. Soon it was all my fault. She was barking in my ear, 'How could you do this to me?' By the time I pushed my way through the crowd four stops early there was no question in anyone's mind who I was. I was the cruel deceiver, the callous brute, the one to blame.

By now the man in combat fatigues had advanced towards me, finger still outstretched. He jabbed it into my chest.

'You anti-capitalist?' he asked.

'Well . . .'

'And anti-monarchist?'

'Ah, in a way . . .'

'If you are anti-capitalist and anti-monarchist then we can talk. Otherwise,' he said, 'it will be difficult. I want to talk to you,' he added. He started rubbing the lapel of my jacket between his thumb and forefinger. Edward was pulling at my sleeve.

'We have to go and meet someone,' he said. The man in combat fatigues took no notice.

'Are you suffering from mental clarity?' he asked me. Here at least the ground was firmer.

'No,' I said.

'No?' He was clearly surprised. He needed a moment or two to take it in. 'Why not?'

'Well, I've always been rather a confused sort of person.'

'That's bad,' he said. And quite suddenly, as if a switch had been flicked, he lost his temper. His hands tightened around my lapels and his voice rose several octaves. 'You must suffer from mental clarity,' he shouted. His friends at the bar who had been paying little attention before now called out to him in a placatory sort of way.

'Mental clarity,' he shouted again. 'You've got to have it.' But this time he sounded less angry. Then he smiled, a broad gap-toothed grin and took his hands off me. He backed away to the bar, still grinning.

'Come on,' said Edward. 'Let's go and eat.'

'Are you worthy of the name of Abraham?' shouted the man. His friends were trying to lift him back on to his bar stool.

'Don't pay any attention,' said Edward. 'There are some very strange people round here.'

We were having lunch with a French Secret Service agent called Philippe. He had recently returned to Kampala after several months

60

away. It was well known that he worked for the French Secret Service. Indeed, almost everyone seemed to know it. People would call out to him in the street asking him who he'd been spying on recently. This annoyed him intensely, and he would go to exhaustive lengths to explain how he was simply an engineer devoted to the rebuilding of Uganda. It didn't make any difference, no one believed him.

Every so often a man in a long white coat came out of the kitchen and hurried to the bar. He would have a quick drink and then hurry back. His coat was spattered with bloodstains. Strangulated squawks and the sound of heavy grunting emerged from the kitchen whenever the door swung open. Philippe was late. Edward and I settled down to read the Ugandan papers.

There were a great many of these. Edward edited the biggest selling national paper, but a vast number of papers and periodicals also came out with varying degrees of regularity. Many were no more than xeroxed broadsheets representing the myriad political factions in the country. Some political groups only numbered two or three members. People often hedged their bets and belonged to several groups at once. Mergers, takeovers and schisms happened all the time. It was hard for anyone to keep up. There was only one common link: everyone was desperate for any form of publicity or recognition.

This was apt to manifest itself in unusual ways. 'Look at this,' said Edward, pointing at the front page of one of the better known weeklies. There was a story that began, 'A previously unknown group has disclaimed responsibility for the grenade attack that killed a Libyan diplomat last week.' The practice had really caught on. Now whenever anything in the least newsworthy happened, representatives of quite unknown groups would issue strongly worded communiqués insisting that they'd had nothing to do with it.

There were further complications to trip up the uninformed. Due to financial difficulties the *Evening News* now only came out once a week, thus making it the world's only weekly evening paper. And for reasons no one could explain the *Sunday Review* was published on a Friday.

Philippe arrived. He was a small, rather plump man with a red face and a goatee beard. The breast pocket of his shirt was crammed with documents. There was a French passport jutting out of the top and what looked very much like another passport behind it. He was in a state of great excitement and waved his cheroot about before he sat down. Immediately, he embarked on a long account of why the Americans should assassinate the President of Kenya without fail. 'The most sensible thing to do,' he kept saying. 'So obvious. Everything would be so much easier.'

'Are you volunteering your services, Philippe?' asked Edward.

Philippe smiled. He put his hand on Edward's wrist. 'I am a man of peace as you know,' he said. 'But sometimes precipitate action is the only way forward.'

I found myself thinking of *She*. Philippe didn't look like a Rider Hagard fan, but it was always difficult to tell. Speculation about other people's reading habits was as haphazard as speculation about the quality, if not the nature, of their sex lives. The latter, in particular, seemed one of the very few lessons of age. Whenever you thought you were right, you were almost invariably wrong.

Certainly, Philippe and Ayesha, while showing no signs of having anything else remotely in common, shared a similar political outlook – a taste for ruthless expediency and an utter disregard for the right of each country to govern itself.

There is a passage in the book where Leo and Holly, having struck up quite a friendship with She, are extolling the virtues of England – the orderliness, the little picket fences, the domestic amenities. She is rather taken with this. So much so that she devises a plan that will enable them all to stick together while she expands her empire. Like all great plans, it has a central incisive thrust. She will come to England and simply take over the throne. Leo and Holly are appalled. They try to explain that England already has a monarch.

'It is naught. It is naught,' said Ayesha; 'she can be overthrown.'

Further plaintive blathering from Holly, along predictably liberal lines, only hardens her resolve. '"The law!" She laughed with scorn " – the law. Canst thou not understand O Holly that I am above the law."'

Philippe beckoned us forward. 'Have you heard, Libyans have been spotted in Kampala. Libyan agents. I have seen them myself.'

'What are they doing here?' asked Edward.

Philippe shrugged. 'I don't know. But it is very worrying for me.'

'Why for you, particularly?'

'I am concerned about my engineering work,' he said.

There was nothing unusual in being fearful of Libyans. Europeans, in particular, were very prone to it. The merest suggestion of a Libyan presence was enough to cause widespread unease in Kampala. It was as if dark riders had been spotted, portents of imminent doom. Relations between Uganda and Libya were in fact fairly amicable, but things were apt to change suddenly. While innumerable groups had by now disclaimed responsibility for the bombing of the Libyan diplomat, the real culprits had not yet been caught.

'Of course,' said Philippe, brightening. 'It might just be something to do with the beans.'

A month earlier Uganda had exported 30 million dollars worth of beans to Libya as part of a barter deal. The news had caused much amusement in Kampala. What did the Libyans want with such a quantity of beans? It was, people said, enough to keep the entire country in a state of sustained flatulence for years. But the Libyans were apparently delighted with their beans, there was even talk of their wanting more.

'I hope it is the beans,' said Philippe. He looked very pensive, fingering one of the passports in his top pocket. 'Let's change the subject,' he said. 'I have just come back from Kasese.'

'What were you doing there?' asked Edward.

He waved away the question. Kasese was a small town in the west of Uganda where Edward and I would buy supplies and hire porters for the Mountains of the Moon. It was a popular smuggling centre. Traffic across the border with Zaire was brisk, with smugglers transporting gold, alcohol and medical supplies back and forth.

'I caught the train back,' Philippe said. 'It was a big mistake.' The railway line had not been renovated in years. At least once a month the entire train would fall over when it tried to take one of the bends. Passengers had to get out and lift it back on to the track. Philippe had travelled at night, for some reason riding up in the engine with the driver and his mate. 'It was like a roller coaster,' he said. 'You could see the headlights twisting like a snake. I have not been so frightened in my entire life. Well, not often.'

Enormous precision was required to drive the train. If the driver went slower than 35 m.p.h. It would fall backwards when it came to the slightest uphill stretch. If he went at more than 45 m.p.h. it would fall off the tracks. On Philippe's previous trip two people had died when the train had fallen over. They had, he said, been crushed quite flat beneath one of the carriages.

He described a big circle in the air with his cheroot. 'Death is everywhere,' he announced grimly. This did not get quite the reaction he wanted. I couldn't help laughing. It sounded absurdly melodramatic. Philippe looked hurt. He turned to Edward and said, 'He does not know yet. He does not know.' Just then the door to the kitchen swung open and the man in the white coat rushed to the bar. But by now his coat was scarcely white at all. There was a large red stain in the middle of his chest, solid in the centre and then breaking up towards the edges. It looked as if someone, or something, had sneezed blood all over him.

That afternoon our pick-up was flagged down as we rode the ruts on the outskirts of Kampala. Edward and I had been to see the tomb of the Kabaka, the last king of Uganda to complete his reign – his son King Freddie was expelled in 1965. A wooden stockade was set on top of a hill and at one end of it was a large conical hut with a thatched roof. Outside there was a girl sitting behind a desk with a few wrinkled postcards on it. She looked astonished to see anyone. There was a notice pinned on the outside of the hut asking visitors to remove their shoes. The girl pointed inside. She did not come in.

In the half-darkness inside two women were sitting knitting on rush mats next to a stuffed leopard in a glass case. On the other side of the hut another woman sat, gazing steadily ahead of her. These were the Kabaka's widows apparently dependent on handouts from the few visitors who went there. As we walked in the two women stopped knitting, raised their arms very slowly as if they were in a trance and extended their hands. There was a faint smell of beef

64

sausages. I placed a couple of notes in an upturned palm. The woman had very long thin fingers, so thin that the flesh fell away on either side of her fingernails. Again very slowly, her fingers curled and clenched over the money. She dropped it into an earthenware pot by her side and did not look up.

Outside the girl was waiting, jabbing her big toe into the dust. The look in her eyes was clear enough. Well, what did you expect, it said. Fireworks? 3D?

A man stood by the side of the road waving furiously with both arms. He was one of the weekly columnists on Edward's paper, a tall middle-aged man dressed in a dark suit and wearing a huge midnight-blue kipper tie. Accidentally shot in the legs a few years earlier, his wife had left him and he had become a severe alcoholic. Now he lived with his mother in his home village outside Kampala and sent in his column to the paper with the men who brought the cows to market.

He sat in the back of the pick-up with me, fidgetting with his clothes. He smelt very strongly of alcohol. His clothes seemed permeated with the stuff. There were even white tide marks on his shoulders, as if he'd gone in for total immersion. After a while he started to cry. The night before he had heard that his daughter had died. She was fifteen and his only child. He had not seen her for a number of years – she lived in the north with her mother. For reasons he didn't yet know – information was still scanty – she had come to Kampala to visit her father and died before she could find him. The cause of death was unknown. There were coils of stubble on his cheeks and his eyes looked puffy. He stared out of the window, his face drawn in a long mark of grief. 'I must try not to cry,' he said. 'But it is very hard.'

We dropped him off at the Ministry of Information. As we pulled away I could see him in the wing mirror standing quite still on the pavement holding on to a lamppost, his feet splayed apart as if he expected the ground to kick and buckle beneath him.

Two days later I ran into Philippe again. He was staying at the Sheraton Hotel, recently reopened after a 26 million dollar refit. The place had fallen derelict during the Amin years and filled up with squatters, who used to heat up their food on bare electric wires. All the money for the refurbishment had come from a barter deal with a Yugoslav construction company. Now Ugandans were stuck with a hotel which charged more than 100 dollars a night for a single room – it was believed to be the most expensive hotel in East Africa. Hardly anyone could afford to stay there – least of all Ugandans. Those who could complained bitterly that they were being ripped off.

The place had only been open for a month. The door man stood outside in a red nylon jacket that was several sizes too big for him and said, 'Have a nice day' to everyone who went in or out. He hadn't got the hang of it yet. He still sounded as if he meant it. Muzak pumped out of concealed speakers in the foyer and the prices in the hotel bar had tripled in the previous week to discourage Ugandans from drinking there.

Philippe was complaining to the receptionist about one of his shirts. It had come back from the laundry minus several buttons. He held it up and indicated the little tufts of cotton where the buttons had been. The receptionist shook her head and suggested that he wear T-shirts in future. Philippe was not pleased. 'I am the sort of man who needs more formal attire,' he said.

When he saw me he grabbed my arm and propelled me towards the front door. 'I have seen more Libyans,' he whispered. 'At least eight or nine.'

'Have you found out what they are doing here?'

'No one will tell me,' he said. 'It is very frustrating. Have you seen them?'

'I don't know.' I said. 'What do they look like?'

He stared at me, was about to say something and then changed his mind. In the end he said, 'You should remember what I told you.' Once again his hand floated towards his breast pocket, more crammed with documents than ever. It was a kind of reflex action, like the way that the old and bedridden pluck convulsively at their eiderdowns.

'About what?'

'This is a dangerous country.'

He dropped my arm and started running down the drive to the main road. For a moment I thought of following him. But I'd begun to lose patience with Philippe. By then he'd advocated a whole series of top-level assassination attempts. There was scarcely an African leader that he hadn't marked down for imminent execution. It seemed inconceivable that he was really a Secret Service agent. Surely the French weren't that desperate?

I wondered if it was all a ploy to invest himself with a bit of mystery. There was a lot to be said for this, of course. Embellishing one's character still had its attractions whatever the pitfalls. In Kampala everyone seemed to be at it, especially the Europeans, many of whom became very cagey when questioned too closely about their reasons for being there. For Philippe the attractions of cloaking himself in subterfuge were ample. His curiosity value was high. Apparently, he was a great success with women, some of whom at least must have been won over by his reputation as a spy.

That afternoon I was at Edward's house packing up my things; we were leaving for the mountains in the morning. Moses, Edward's office driver was siphoning petrol out of a drum into the pick-up. He was going to drive us as far as Kasese. The road was said to be bad, heavy rains had washed away the tarmac surface in places and there had been reports of bandits holding up vehicles. A turkey stood by the garage door leaning its head on one of the supports, watching as Moses sucked the petrol up the siphon tube to get the flow going. No one else was around.

A man on a moped rattled the padlock on the gate. 'Please let me in,' he said. 'I am a friend of Edward's.' I swung back one of the gates and he wheeled his moped inside.

'How are you?' he asked.

'I am fine, thank you,' I said. 'How are you?'

'I am not very well,' he said. 'Please excuse me for not being more cheerful, but my wife died last week. She got cerebral malaria and two days later she was dead. I went out of our bedroom for two minutes just to get her something to drink and when I came back she had passed away. She was lying propped up on the pillows looking at the door, waiting for me to come back. But she hadn't been able to hold on. I closed her eyes and knelt by the bed to pray that her soul would go to heaven.

'Life is very hard,' he said. 'Now I don't know what to do. You see, I was living steady-style, I had no other women. I suppose I must try to find another woman. But it is not easy. You can't just go into town and pick up a woman, not one you want to live with. Time is very slow for me. At night I lie in our bed and I can't go to sleep. Sometimes I go to sleep for a little while and then when I wake up I think she's still beside me. I would rather not sleep at all than have that feeling. I just try to stay away from my home and work all the time so I don't get bored and think about what has happened to me. Now I am going to see everyone I can think of in order to keep my mind busy.'

'I am very sorry to hear about your wife,' I said.

'Thank you. I am grateful for your concern.' He held out his hand. I took it and we shook hands for a while. Then he turned his moped round and wheeled it back out of the gate. Outside in the road he sat astride the bike, paddling his feet along the ground until the motor caught.

Six

The sound of screaming rose from downstairs, a thin high-pitched wail broken by flurries of equally agonised shrieks. There was a knock on the bedroom door. 'I am waiting to enter your room,' said Edward. Two years in Uganda had done strange things to Edward's diction. Ugandans tended to speak to one another in a slow, precise, rather archaic sort of way. When they were being formal, conversations could proceed along almost liturgical lines, a series of ritual exchanges inviting the appropriate responses. The habit was catching.

'Why are you waiting to enter my room?'

'I have a cup of tea.'

'Be so good as to enter.'

Edward came in. The screaming from downstairs grew louder, even higher pitched. It was the sort of noise that can dissolve bone marrow.

'What the hell is that?'

'That,' said William, 'is "Ave Maria". It's the only recording ever made of a castrato. He was almost seventy at the time. Fantastic breath control. I always play it when I'm about to embark on anything big.'

Outside it was starting to get light, a broadening band of grey across the horizon. Birds were stirring in the garden. In England this would have consisted of some modest twittering, a whirring of tiny wings as the birds went about their ablutions. In Uganda it was as if the trees had suddenly sprung to life. Huge dark shapes detached themselves from the branches and wheeled about in search of any stray livestock with which to start their day. We loaded up the pick-up. There was enough dried food to keep us going for months, rattling boxes full of dehydrated meals designed to be cooked at high altitude. They came with helpful little labels like, 'While the instant mashed potato can be cooked in the same pan as the instant goulash it is psychologically more uplifting to serve them separately.'

There were almost as many boxes of pills as there were of food. It was a hypochondriac's delight, an entire mobile dispensary. I knew because I gave way to no one in my susceptibility to imaginary diseases. Edward too, while a comparative novice when it came to placebos, was not immune to the attractions of a well-stocked medicine chest. We had antibiotics, sleeping pills, stomach pills, constipation pills, diarrhoea pills, pills to combat altitude sickness and even pills to stop your head from swelling up and exploding.

I was particularly pleased with these last ones. Apparently there was a very slight chance that your brain tissue might swell up at altitude, to such a degree that it ruptured your cranium and sent shards of skull raining down over a large area. My doctor in London had explained this to me. He said the chances of it happening were remote. 'I would say five thousand, no, ten thousand to one.' By then he had already written out a thick sheaf of presciptions. I was holding things up, the waiting room was getting congested. 'Do you really want these?' he said. 'They're quite unnecessary.'

But the time had long since passed when I took chances with odds of ten thousand to one. There were meteorites out there with my name inscribed on them.

'How many can you let me have?' I said.

The doctor sighed and wrote out another prescription. 'Take two if your hat size increases,' he said.

I made sure that the tub of Joe Weider's Dynamic Carbo-Energiser had been packed. It was wedged into the top of one of the rucksacks, Joe's enraged tangerine gleam already visible in the half-light. Moses had loaded a full drum of petrol on to the pick-up. The petrol crisis had now overtaken the beer crisis. More than half the petrol stations in Uganda were dry, even the black market was running low. You had to travel with your own supplies. The only trouble was that carrying conspicuous drums of petrol laid you open to the risk of attack from other motorists, stranded without fuel and out to revenge themselves on those who had managed to stay mobile.

It was a long day's drive to Kasese, if the bandits didn't get us, the petrol lasted and the road was still there. We would spend two days in Kasese, hiring porters and buying further supplies before setting out. That was assuming the weather stayed fine. There were only two brief periods in the year when it was safe to go walking in the Mountains of the Moon. The rest of the time it rained incessantly, turning the whole area into an enormous impassable bog. But it was getting harder and harder to predict when the dry spells would be. The climate was changing, things no longer happened when they were supposed to. The year before more rain had fallen during one of the dry spells than in any other month.

Edward looked exhilarated. He walked round the pick-up several times checking that everything was wedged in securely and slapping the petrol drum with the flat of his hand. 'This is it,' he said. 'The start of our big adventure. How do you feel?'

How did I feel? The more I thought about it, the more inadvisable this whole thing seemed. What did I expect to find? The Kingdom of Kôr? 'A white sorceress in the heart of an African swamp?' The eighty-five copper statues from whose mouths the Nile gushed forth? There was a fundamental clash between fantasy and reality here; the chances of tying the two together looked hopeless.

'What are you doing?' asked Edward.

'What do you mean?'

'Your jaw was quivering. It looked as if you were nibbling lettuce. Are you ready?'

Moses started the engine. We pulled out into Baskerville Drive, skirted Castration Corner and took the road west. And thus, as Horace C. Holly had put it, in rather different circumstances – typically, he was quite untroubled by anything in the way of doubts – 'began our search for the ruined city and the Fire of Life'.

The sun was coming up now. On the outskirts of the city a steady stream of men on bicycles rode to work. Several had bundles of sugar-cane lashed to the backs of their bikes. Mist still hung over the papyrus swamps, swirling and trailing off in wisps as the air grew warmer. Moses weaved his way through the ranks of cyclists, banging the horn to alert the unwary. His sun-hat was crammed down over his head. He held the steering wheel cradled in his palms, as a water diviner might hold his stick, poised for the slightest vibration or pull to left or right.

Moses was renowned as one of the best drivers in Kampala. During the war – the last war – he had been with the guerillas in the bush tending the vehicles. Army commanders vied for his services. They knew they got a smooth ride with Moses. However, eventual victory had done nothing to boost Moses' opinion of the moral character of his countrymen. 'Ugandan cheats,' he said repeatedly, half to himself. 'Ugandan thieves everywhere.' As far as he was concerned the whole population was blighted by uncontrollable avarice. Even he wasn't immune. Their depravity was likely to rub off on him if he didn't take care. Fortunately, he said, he had found God, so there was a slim prospect of his staying unscathed.

The road ran through fields of matoke, short, stubby trees with huge green leaves and branches bent double under the weight of clusters of green bananas. Just as the moral failings of Ugandans were one of the main preoccupations of Moses' life, so matoke was the other. Few westerners took to the stuff, not without extensive practice anyway. It's usually cooked by being steamed in its own leaves and served in thick yellow slabs like atrophied custard, a kind of extraordinary fibrous mashed potato with a bland, faintly bitter taste. But Ugandans, who consume more fibre than any other race in the world, invest matoke with an almost mystical significance. None more so than Moses.

Occasionally we would stop, while he admired a particularly fetching bunch of matoke. He would describe the synchronicity of the branches, the angle at which the fruit sprang from the central stem, the general line of curvature.

'You won't find anyone who knows more about matoke than Moses,' said Edward admiringly.

We stopped too at various roadside stalls selling great piles of matoke branches. There was no intention of buying anything. The stops were simply so that Moses could check the prices being asked and thus reassure himself that the level of Ugandan venality had not peaked or suffered any unaccountable blips. He was never disappointed. Each time he would stand looking incredulously at the stallholder, repeating 'You terrible Ugandan cheat.' The stallholders didn't look in the least upset. A few even looked rather pleased, shouting proudly at other neighbouring stallholders who had missed out on the full force of Moses' disapproval.

By the side of the road bombed out tanks and armoured cars sat rusting in the dust. We passed the Equator, marked by two huge hoops of concrete on either side of the road that looked as if they'd been built to carry a vast electrical cable girding the Earth. Up ahead here was an army pick-up carrying a load of rebel prisoners – the army was still mopping up dissident groups in the north. They had surrendered and were en route to re-education camp where they'd be lectured for the next few months on the folly of their ways.

The lorry was packed. The men were stripped to the waist, wearing only brown cotton trousers. They gazed disconsolately over the tailgate. A soldier stood at the front of the pick-up, keeping watch over them. His rifle was slung over his shoulder and he was chewing gum. The chances of anyone trying to escape were remote. The prisoners all knew that they'd probably be killed by the first people they met. There wasn't much sympathy for rebels round here.

The soldier waved as we pulled out to overtake. He pointed at the prisoners and shouted something. From the look on his face it must have been a joke, but his words were blown away. We pulled ahead, Moses urged the pick-up on, chanting invocations under his breath. On the crests of the hills the air shimmered where the heat bounced off the tarmac. I wound the window fully down, cupped my hand and let the wind drag it backwards, bouncing on the gusts.

There was something else, another persistent itch flaring up. For years I had dreamed of going on a journey. Not just a simple haul from A to B. But something big, epic even – I was apt to get carried away on a crescendo of adjectives here – heroic. This too had been fuelled by books, mostly American Beat novels from the 1950s. Books whose heroes frenziedly crisscrossed the country, driven onwards by benzedrine and high hopes. Never drawing breath as the mileometer keeps spinning round.

I was eighteen, sitting in my bedroom on the edge of the southern commuter belt and it was as if a giant gust of wind had just got under the carpet. This was more like it. I was looking for something that would enable me to make the big leap from adolescence to adulthood, from timidity to exuberance. Here it was, a way of gouging out some imprint for yourself, of letting people know you'd arrived. High-octane, purposeless travelling held the key; the abandon, the irre-sponsibility, the self-destruction.

I was very taken with this. Letting people know I had arrived was quite an obsession. I wanted to run up to strangers on the street and announce, 'Don't worry. I made it. It's all right.' But this sort of behaviour was frowned upon in England. It didn't go down at all well. So I went to America. There it was actively encouraged.

'The only ones for me are the mad ones, the ones who are mad to live, mad to talk, mad to be saved, desirous of everything at the same time, the ones who never yawn or say a commonplace thing, but burn, burn, burn like fabulous yellow roman candles,' Jack Kerouac had written in *On the Road*. Every time I read this surges of excitement went through me. Yes, yes, I thought. Me too. But America wasn't what it was cracked up to be. The fabulous roman candles had all moved to Mexico. Instead, the country was full of greasy truck drivers who showed you photographs of their wives and children, told you how happily married they were, and then tried to vault the men's room partitions to catch a glimpse of your private parts. And they were the docile ones.

I put America aside. But the hankerings persisted, way beyond the point when they should have faded discreetly away. I couldn't bear to read *On the Road* anymore. I would wrinkle up with embarrassment whenever I opened it. The over-writing, the awful cloying romanti-cism. Besides, I had met a few of these fabulous roman candles by now. They were nothing to aspire to, hopeless narcissists raving with mental ill-discipline. But I couldn't quite shake off the pangs. They were like tugs on a curtain that opened to reveal a familiar scene – the endless road unrolling into the night.

74

There were certain ground rules for this kind of thing. Mythic travel had its conventions. For a start you needed a companion – the grim spectre of buddy-bonding took a bow here. And then the chemistry had to be just right, the interplay between the two up front. Both needed to be avid seekers after sensation, unfettered by anything in the way of caution. If you faltered, you were lost. I had tried to convince myself that Edward and I had what it took to scorch a distinctive furrow across the map and write ourselves into the hothead handbook. But it was heavy going. At every major hurdle we tripped headlong into ignominy. Any hopes that we might still make it had taken what threatened to be a final knock two years earlier.

It was my first trip to Africa. Edward was en route to Uganda for the second time where he was going to join up again with the guerrillas in the bush. We flew to Mombassa, found a hotel by the sea, and on the first evening went looking for a drink. There were hotels all the way up the beach, hidden behind straggling clumps of eucalyptus. Most had signs outside announcing that they served Wiener Schnitzel – Mombassa was very popular with Germans. The bar we chose was full of them, middle-aged men in sports shirts chuckling in slurred voices. The barman wore what looked like Moslem dress without the flat hat, and served drinks with an expression of deep disapproval scored on his face.

Around the walls were banquettes covered in red velvet. We sat at the bar on overstuffed mushroom stools. It was difficult to keep your balance without holding on to something. Several of the other drinkers were having problems, swaying uncertainly as they made periodic lunges for their glasses.

'Look,' said Edward.

'Look at what?'

'Look behind you.'

I turned round. Two African girls were sitting on one of the banquettes. Their hair was plaited and threaded through with different coloured beads. One of them was wearing a very short skirt and lurex tights. The other glanced at me and stuck her tongue under her lower lip as if she was sluicing her gums.

'Do you see them?'

'You mean the girls?'

Edward sighed in exasperation. 'Of course I mean the girls. What do you think?'

'I don't know. All right, I suppose.'

'Better than all right. You know what they are?'

It was sufficient to look momentarily confused for Edward to pitch in with the answer. 'Bar girls. You see them all over East Africa. Good time girls, you must have heard the expression.'

I looked at the girls again and pretended to be studying the poster behind them when they both stared back. It offered safari trips and showed a photograph of an overweight man in bush hat and shorts, apparently on the verge of collapse.

'Are they prostitutes?'

The distinction was clearly a difficult one. Edward shrugged and made alternative weighing motions with his hands. 'Sometimes. Not really. They don't always do it for the money, but they expect something in return.'

'Like what?'

'Well, just a token. Clothes, that sort of thing. They don't like to go away empty-handed. The thing is,' he said, 'that apparently they enjoy it. It's not just business. They actually get a big kick out of sleeping with white men.'

'Are you speaking from experience?'

Edward shook his head vigorously, then seemed struck by the thought that this might be rather priggish and slowed his rate of shaking. 'No, but these things are common knowledge round here. What do you think? We could go and talk to them.'

'Could we?'

'Of course. They're probably expecting it.' Edward sounded very earnest. He was almost hissing.

'I don't know,' I said. 'Buy me another drink.'

Edward rummaged in the pockets of his trousers. He sunk his hands in until the material was half way up his forearms, and then he slapped his back pocket.

'I've left my money behind. Shit. It must be in the hotel. Have you got enough?'

76

I took out my wallet and we inspected the little wad of notes. I held up one of them to attract the barman's attention. It was damp with sweat and flopped over on to my fingers. The barman stared at it and went on serving the Germans.

There was a tap on my shoulder. At first I thought it was Edward. Then I turned round and saw the girl who had been sluicing her gums. She smiled at us. There were gaps between each of her teeth.

'Hello,' she said.

'Hello.'

'Hi,' said Edward.

'Would you like to come and sit with us?'

'I don't know,' I said. 'Would we?'

Edward exhaled a little shudder of air and gave the barest of nods. Without moving his lips he said, 'Buy them drinks.'

'Can I get you something to drink?'

'Two beers, please.'

The barman pulled the tops off four bottles of beer with undue ferocity and slid them across the bar. He slapped the change down as if it was burning his hand. Edward and I took the drinks over to the banquette. The girl from the bar stood aside to let Edward slide in next to her friend. She then sat down, patting the seat beside her.

There was no doubt that Edward had got the more attractive girl. She was also a lot more lively, launching straight into animated conversation. Mine, after taking a sip of her beer, did nothing apart from nestling her cheek against my arm. I manoeuvred myself as discreetly as possible so that she was no longer leaning against my vaccination marks.

'What's your name?'

'My name is Rosemary,' she said, carefully enunciating each syllable. 'And my friend is called Josephine. What is your name?'

'My name is John.'

This news prompted a surprising reaction. Rosemary snapped out of her reverie and even drew her head away to look at me. 'Really?' she said. Her long index finger pointed at my chin. 'Your name is John?'

'Yes,' I said with relief. Here was what promised to be an

opportunity to make up lost conversational ground on Edward. 'My name is John.'

Rosemary began to laugh incredulously. 'John is my father's name.'

'Is it? Is it really?'

'Look,' said Rosemary. She laid her left arm on the table. On the underside near her wrist was a tattoo. It consisted of a drawing of a house. Over the roof were some hieroglyphics and above those, written in a manner that suggested that the tattooist had barely mastered his craft, or else had been pushed for time, was the word John.

There was a grizzle of laughter from Edward along the banquette. He and Josephine were becoming entwined. Rosemary nodded approvingly and hooked her foot over mine.

'What would you like to do?' she asked.

'I don't know. What are the choices?'

'You could come to the club with us.'

'Maybe.'

'Only maybe? Don't you like me?'

'Yes. I like you.' And then, because something else seemed called for and nothing suitably non-commital came to mind, I said, 'Of course I like you.'

'So we go to the club then.'

'Perhaps.'

Much the same conversation, although conducted in a vastly higher gear, must have been going on between Edward and Josephine. Edward lent across the table, upsetting some beer on to Josephine's tights. They both dabbed at it with paper napkins. 'Do you want to go to the club?' said Edward.

'What do you think?'

He lowered his voice. 'I wouldn't mind. Trouble is, what about the money? How much have you got?'

'How much do you think it will be?'

'No idea. We could just go to the club, though. That wouldn't commit us to anything.'

The club was only reachable by taxi, but there turned out to be a taxi driver sitting at the next table. As we walked out Rosemary took my hand. The four of us climbed into the back of the taxi with the two girls in the middle. For some minutes it looked as if the car wouldn't start. The driver sat hunched over the steering wheel, fiddling under the dashboard. He was trying to start the car by touching two of the engine leads together. The engine turned in a mournful sort of way, but wouldn't catch. Just as we sat resignedly back in our seats, it burst into life.

We drove up the dirt track to the main road. On either side of the narrow ribbon of tarmac palm trees jutted up into the night sky. The car had no suspension. Whenever we hit a bump we would be thrown into the air and then fall back on to the cracked plastic upholstery. After about ten minutes the car pulled off the road and down another dirt track. There was a sentry-box at the end. A man in a cap touched his peak at us and raised a long white pole.

The club was attached to a hotel. Slatted wooden sunbeds were scattered around on the grass. The man on the door seemed to know the girls, who promptly started haggling over the entrance fee. Edward and I stood to one side as negotiations took place. 'They're certainly economically sound,' he said. Eventually it was decided that the four of us would pay the normal price of admission for one person. The man opened the door and with a grand sweeping gesture ushered us in.

The ground dropped away beneath me. I plunged forward and was prevented from falling by a hand that grabbed the back of my shirt collar and hung on as I toppled. In the darkness I could just make out Rosemary, her separated teeth hanging suspended above me.

'You didn't see the step?' she asked.

'No.'

As my eyes grew used to the gloom I saw there were only two other guests in the club. Both were elderly men and they looked up excitedly at the new arrivals, before returning to their drinks.

At the bar I ordered four more beers. There was some confusion over the seating arrangements. After some discussion Edward and I ended up on the outside two barstools with the girls in between.

Rosemary sucked at the top of her beer bottle without lifting it from the bar.

'It's quiet in here.'

'Yes,' she said. 'It's nice.'

Edward gave a loud yelp, which was followed by a burst of giggling from Josephine. He got off his stool and came over. While it was hard to tell in the dark, he seemed to have reddened, as if a sudden rush of blood had distended his features.

'Why did you scream?'

'She put her hand on my parts.'

'On your what?'

'On my parts. She reached out and grabbed them.'

'Is that standard practice?'

'I don't know. Came as quite a shock though. What do you think of yours?'

'Not much.'

Edward was staring at Rosemary, moving his head back and forth, trying to settle on an optimum angle.

'I see what you mean. She looks as if she's been around a bit. Mine's younger, don't you think? I'm quite tempted.'

'Are you?'

'I'm not sure.'

The record ended. A new one started. The volume had been turned up. Josephine took Edward's hand and pulled him towards the dance-floor.

'We dance too,' said Rosemary.

'All right.'

On the dance-floor Edward was making efforts to keep his body in time with the music. He swung his arms and lifted his feet in a manner that suggested he was being convulsed by intermittent electric shocks. Josephine was rendered almost immobile by this display. She stood, swaying her hips, her mouth hanging half open.

'Your friend is a good dancer,' said Rosemary.

'Do you think so?'

'Oh yes. European style.'

For a moment I wondered whether to follow Edward's example. I decided against it, choosing instead to dance in as laconic and casual a way as possible. Every so often I clicked the fingers of my left hand in vague approximation to the beat. The next record was slow. Rosemary moved in for the clinch. We set off awkwardly, shuffling round the perimeter of the dance-floor, trying to hang on to the basic conventions of a waltz step. Edward was being borne in the opposite direction, his head hanging lifelessly over Josephine's shoulder. As the last note died away I disentangled myself and headed back to the bar.

'You don't want to dance anymore?' said Rosemary.

'A little later perhaps.'

'It's OK, the show will begin soon.'

'What show?'

Rosemary gestured at the rostrum. 'Very good show. You'll like it.'

Edward was already seated at the bar. He had ordered four more beers. Now there were eight bottles ranged along the counter.

'We're going to have to make up our minds soon,' he said. 'What do you reckon?'

'I'm not very keen.'

'You haven't changed your mind?'

'Not really.'

Edward opened and closed his mouth a few times without saying anything. Then he said, 'I'm not sure either. I'm tempted. It's just that I'm a bit worried about disease. Apparently the American navy was here recently.'

'What, all of it?'

'Not all, but quite a few ships.'

'Hey,' said Josephine, rattling her foot against the legs of Edward's stool. 'You must talk to me.'

In the lavatory one of the elderly men was standing by the mirror and examining his hair. He took out a comb and experimented with several different partings, holding up strands of hair and sighing as he let them fall back on to his scalp. The bowl of each urinal was full of little white balls of disinfectant. I wished I was back at the hotel, my stomach felt blown up with lager gas. I wrung my hands together unhappily under the hot air blower.

Four new beers stood on the bar. Edward had given up using a glass and was drinking straight from the bottle. There was a roll of drums from the two speakers and the lights dimmed even more. 'It's the show,' whispered Rosemary.

She held my hand, rubbing my knuckles with the inside of her thumb. Her skin was dry and heavily calloused. Two men dressed in tribal costume, carrying spears and shields covered in animal skin leaped on to the rostrum. They banged the blunt ends of their spears on the floor several times before leaning them carefully against the back wall.

Another man with his body oiled and wearing only a loin-cloth, ran up on to the rostrum and dived into the arms of his two companions. He bowed at the empty tables and chairs.

'God I hate this sort of thing,' said Edward. 'It's cultural prostitution.'

'Steady on.'

Edward clapped his hand over his mouth and glanced at the girls. But they were preoccupied with the show and had moved out from behind the beer bottles to get a better look. The man in the loin-cloth lay on the floor and performed feats of contortion. He leaned over backwards and stuck his head through his legs, grinning fixedly as his ears brushed between his knees. The two men in tribal costume stood on either side like conjuror's assistants, describing patterns in the air with their shields at the end of each trick.

'It's very good,' said Rosemary.

'Haven't you seen it before?' I asked.

'Oh yes,' she said. 'But it gets better.'

Three women appeared and jumped over one another in a desultory sort of way. There was a fanfare. The two warriors leaped on to the shoulders of the three women and stood there, swaying. The man in the loin-cloth managed to scramble up one side of the pyramid and, after much grunting and a hastily suppressed howl of pain, he ascended the summit. There was a brief moment when the edifice was quite still, and then it began to shake violently. The man in the loin-cloth looked alarmed. He jumped to the ground just as one of the warriors lost his footing on the shoulder of the women

82

beneath. Disaster had been narrowly averted. Rosemary and Josephine clapped enthusiastically.

'Awful,' said Edward. 'Just awful.'

Josephine snuggled up against his shoulder. Edward pulled away and sat staring gloomily in front of him. Josephine looked at him in surprise and then backed slowly off into the dark.

Less than a minute later she reappeared at the other end of the bar with her arm round the man who had been grooming himself in the lavatory. His hair was now combed straight down his forehead and levelled off to one side just above his eyebrows. He was delighted with the success of his new hairstyle and kept up a steady stream of giggles as Josephine stood talking with her mouth close to his ear.

'Looks like I've blown it,' said Edward.

'Do you want to go?'

'You're still all right, though.'

'No, it's OK. I don't mind. Really.'

'What's happening?' said Rosemary, digging me in the ribs.

'I think we're going to go.'

She gave a long moan of disappointment that only petered out when she had to take another breath.

'Why? You must stay for the second show.'

'I don't think so.'

Rosemary grasped my wrists and turned me round to face her. 'You don't want to take me home?'

'Not tonight.'

'We could go on the beach. It's nice on the sand.'

'Some other time.'

She did not blink for a while. 'All right,' she said. 'I will go too.'

'But we are going back to our hotel.'

'No,' she said. 'I mean I will go to my home.'

She looked at Josephine who now had her thumb under the man's fringe and was lifting it up inquisitively. I called for the bill. The barman wrote out a long column of figures and began adding them up. It came to more money than I had on me.

'What are we going to do?' I said to Edward.

'I don't know.'

'We haven't got enough money.'

'I know.'

'What's the matter?' said Rosemary.

'We haven't got enough money,' said Edward.

'No?' she said. 'I will pay.' She undid the clasp of her bag, pulled out some notes and laid them on the bar. I put my hand on hers.

'No, really, you can't.'

Rosemary removed my hand and put it beside the notes. 'It's OK,' she said. 'I am a good business girl.'

The doorman tipped his cap as we went out and pointed at the tarmac strip where another taxi stood waiting with its back doors open. Edward and I strode on towards the sentry-box and the white pole.

'Hey,' shouted Rosemary. 'Where are you going?'

'We'll walk,' called Edward.

The taxi drew up alongside us. Rosemary opened the back door and patted the seat. 'We will take you home,' she said. 'It's all right.'

Edward tripped as he climbed through the door and fell towards Rosemary. She helped him into an upright position. I couldn't close the door properly. The driver had to lean over and jiggle with the lock mechanism. It was the same man who had been performing contortions in the floor show. Once he had fixed the door he remained twisted round looking at us and talking to Rosemary in Swahili.

We bumped up the dirt track to the main road. When we reached the turn-off to our hotel, I said, 'You can drop us off here if you like.' Neither the driver nor Rosemary took any notice.

There was a light bulb hanging from a flag pole and swinging about in the breeze. Fruit bats dived back and forth through the arbor that led to the front door.

'Maybe we meet again tomorrow,' said Rosemary.

'Very possibly,' said Edward. 'Will you be in the same place?'

'Of course.'

'And Josephine?'

She smiled and raised one shoulder slightly. I started to explain how we could pay her back the money we owed her, but she cut me off. 'It's not important.'

We wished them goodnight. 'I have enjoyed meeting you,' said Rosemary. The driver looked at Rosemary and then nodded enthusiastically, as if to dispel any doubts that might have been around. The taxi pulled away, spitting pebbles behind it.

'I feel bad,' said Edward.

'So do I. I feel humiliated.'

'Do you? I'm not sure if I feel that bad.'

We had forgotten to light the mosquito coils in the bedroom. There was a low hum of insect activity that dropped momentarily when we opened the door and then resumed. We lay on our beds while the mosquitoes massed for attack.

'Do you think we should go back tomorrow?' said Edward.

'No.'

'You don't think they'd be pleased to see us?'

'No.'

Outside the waves swept up and down the beach. Someone was snoring in the room next door.

'No,' said Edward, after a while. 'Nor do I.'

You see? How can you hope to join the immortals after behaviour like this? Of course, there were ample reasons for playing safe. But somehow that wasn't the point. Somehow it still amounted to a failure of nerve. The great joyriders had left us far behind. The only thing for it was to settle back and take in the view.

The matoke had disappeared. Moses had fallen silent, there was nothing of interest for him here. Now the hills were dry and pink and crowned with clusters of mud huts. It was easy to remember that Uganda had once been proposed as the Promised Land. In the late 1940s various sites were put forward by the British for the new State of Israel. One of the plans was that parts of Uganda and Sudan should be lumped together and turned into a Jewish homeland. But the plan didn't go down at all well with the Jews, who had set their sights on Palestine and were not about to be fobbed off with an obscure chunk of East Africa. No one had taken much notice of what the Ugandans and Sudanese thought about it.

'I'm hungry,' said Edward. 'We can have breakfast in Lyantonde. They do a good breakfast there. Unfortunately, that's not all they do.'

'What do you mean?'

'Very sad people in Lyantonde,' said Moses, coming to suddenly and showing a rare concern for his fellow countrymen.

'Very sad,' echoed Edward. 'It's the world capital of AIDS.'

Seven

We parked the pick-up by the Feel at Home Hotel, a blue-painted one-storey building with breeze block castellations running along the roof. There wasn't much to Lyantonde, a single wide street lined on either side with similar one-storey buildings. Most of them were hotels or restaurants. The town was a pick-up stop, somewhere drivers could rest up for a while and grab some recreation if they felt so inclined.

It was the recreation that was the cause of all the trouble. While one in five of the adult population of Kampala were now AIDS carriers, in Lyantonde the figure was nearer one in three. The place had what was believed to be the highest concentration of HIV positives ever recorded. The reasons weren't hard to fathom. Just about all the hotels and restaurants were also brothels. If you liked the look of a waitress then she too could be purchased with your meal. This made getting served in Lyantonde a hazardous business. If someone at another table took a fancy to your waitress then she could disappear without warning and your order would get trapped in limbo until she returned.

At the Salina Hotel next to the Feel at Home Hotel there was a little verandah that stuck out into the dirt. It was surrounded by iron palings on which white net curtains had been pinned. Moses insisted that we ate our breakfast no more than 10 feet away from the pick-up. Any further and there was a risk that we could be outsprinted by the snatch thieves who, he assured us, were at that moment tweaking the net curtains on the other side of the street and eyeing up the pick-up.

The waitress took our order. She was a big girl, no more than about sixteen, dressed in a cotton frock printed with forget-me-knots. Edward and I ordered eggs. Moses was already waiting eagerly for his first matoke of the day. I went inside to look for somewhere to pee. The woman behind the counter waved me towards the back and said something about a wall. It sounded as if there was a specially designated wall to pee against. But once outside, it looked as if you could choose any wall available and not set much of a precedent.

A square of dried earth was surrounded on all sides by once whitewashed shacks. I thought for a while that they must keep horses. Stable doors with numbers stencilled on them opened out on all sides. It took some time for me to realise that this was where the pick-up drivers brought the waitresses to round off their meals. The door to one of the horseboxes was ajar. Inside was a metal bed, a foam mattress and a nastily compacted looking pile of bedding.

As I was choosing my spot, another of the horseboxes opened and a couple came out. The man looked thoroughly pleased with himself, smiling at me and clapping the girl on the shoulder in a comradely sort of way. She looked less pleased, cramming herself back into her dress and hurrying back inside to resume her waitress duties. The man stretched and tucked his shirt into his trousers.

'First time in Lyantonde?' he said.

I admitted that it was.

'Very nice place,' he said. 'Very friendly.'

AIDS awareness may have been making gradual inroads into the rest of Uganda, but in Lyantonde it hadn't got anywhere. There wasn't even a 'Beware the Sweetness and Splendour of Sex' poster to be seen. Local doctors and foreign specialists had tried to persuade the girls and the drivers of the virtues of condoms, but they weren't having any of it. Other small towns in the area had to subsist on agriculture and occasional bits of light industry. In Lyantonde business was booming. Prostitution was the lifeblood of the local economy. Most of the girls started young, often in their early teens. They worked hard for a few years, saved some money and turned themselves into attractive marriage prospects.

Meanwhile the drivers kept coming through, contracting AIDS and spreading it further up and down the line. By the time the first symptoms appeared, the memory of a quick tumble in a Lyantonde horsebox would have long since faded.

The waitress brought our food. Moses prodded his plate of matoke

88

and looked unhappy. He twisted his plate round to get a full panoramic view of it. Very gingerly he took his first bite. It was, he conceded in obvious astonishment, rather good. The scrambled eggs were the yellowest I had ever seen, the colour of mustard in full bloom.

At the next table was a man in the latter stages of AIDS. He was very thin and moved with difficulty, as if his joints were giving him pain. All around his neck there were small matt black contusions that stood out from the general shininess of his skin. These were Kaposi's Sarcoma, the first indication that your immune system has started to break down. The waitress came to take his order. He wanted a cup of tea and some eggs, but when the eggs arrived his appetite had disappeared. He cut them up and pushed them around the plate but ate virtually nothing. The waitress tried to persuade him to have another go. He shook his head and pushed his plate away.

Beyond Lyantonde, said Moses, the road was very bad. This was not to be taken lightly. When a Ugandan tells you that the road is bad, it usually means that it has long ceased to resemble anything that could remotely be called a road. Very bad was almost unheard of. It wasn't as though the road to Lyantonde had been good. While the government had recently instigated a big new road improvement scheme, few if any repairs had been done in Uganda for more than twenty years. The tarmac crumbled, became pitted or else disappeared altogether, washed away in floods. But, as it turned out, the state of the road wasn't the only problem up ahead.

Just outside Lyantonde there is a road junction where the road that leads through the town joins up with what the very fancifully inclined might call the Lyantonde by-pass. This is a single-track road that skirts the town for the use of those who don't wish to lay themselves open to temptation by driving past the Feel At Home and its many companions. An army pick-up was pulled over to the side of the road. A soldier was sitting on the bonnet peering down the barrel of his gun. He was wearing reflecting aviator sun-glasses. When we stopped I could see Moses' reflection caught in the curve of his lenses, his face stretched to twice its normal width.

'How are things up ahead?' asked Edward.

The soldier put down his gun. 'The situation up ahead,' he said, 'is promising.'

A mile or so further on, three cars were stopped in the middle of the road. People were standing about, apparently in a state of some excitement. One man in particular was waving his arms about and shouting at anyone who would listen. As we drove up he flagged us down.

'We have been held up,' he said. 'There are highwaymen around.'

He introduced himself. 'I am the Minister of State for Foreign Affairs,' he said. He had been riding along in his pick-up with his bodyguard when a number of masked men – estimates varied as to how many – jumped out of the undergrowth and forced them to stop. The Minister's bodyguard, who was riding with him in the backseat, had waved his rifle out of the window at the robbers. The rifle, he admitted to me quietly when no one else was paying attention, was not loaded at the time, due to an oversight on his part. But the sight of a rifle was enough to give the robbers pause for thought. They were undecided whether to stand and fight or make a run for it.

Meanwhile, the Minister's bodyguard was desperately trying to load his rifle. He finally managed to do so and fired several shots at the robbers. This decided them. They turned and fled, but not before one of them had thrown a grenade at the Minister's car. It had bounced off the roof and failed to explode. The Minister had retrieved it as a souvenir. Now it sat in the backseat with the bodyguard, who had shifted as far away from it as possible. But due to the slope of the road surface or the state of the seat, it kept rolling towards him whenever he moved. Understandably reluctant to pick it up and put it somewhere else, he shrank towards the window looking the other way and trying to pretend that it wasn't nudging against his trousers.

The Minister was not pleased. He was talking to the Mayor of Lyantonde who was busy apologising for the lawlessness of the local population. The robbers were believed to be deserters from the

90

army. They had been operating for several weeks and so far had killed two people and set a car on fire.

I couldn't get over the grenade. It looked like something for unblocking drains, a bulbous mushroom top with a wooden stem beneath it. It was the sort of grenade I had seen in war comics at school – not the pineapple types that men called Chalkie and Lofty lobbed at men called Fritz in stiff bowling actions. This was from quite another era. More Boer War than Great War. It belonged to a time of spiked helmets and muskets.

'What do you think?' said Edward.

'Think about what?'

'About going on?'

'I don't know,' I said. 'What do you think?'

'I'm not sure,' said Edward. 'I should think it will be all right.'

'Are you? What makes you think that?'

'The Minister's bodyguard probably scared them off. It's unlikely they'll attack again so soon.'

'It is?'

Edward nodded. He looked very sure of himself. Ahead the road climbed a hill and dropped out of sight. There was no indication what lay beyond.

'You are going on?' asked the Minister.

'Yes,' I said. 'We're both pretty sure that you will have frightened them off.'

The Minister gave this some thought. He put the tips of his fingers together and stared at the ground. 'I think you're probably right,' he said. He didn't sound at all convinced.

We got back into the pick-up. The Minister's bodyguard waved goodbye. But he didn't want to do anything too sudden or expansive on account of the grenade next to him, so it was a rather muted gesture.

As soon as we crossed the brow of the hill the road deteriorated rapidly. It grew steadily narrower with scoops missing from the sides as if something had been taking enormous bites out of the tarmac. Before long there were more potholes than there was road. A lot more. Moses bore down on the potholes, his hands wobbling furiously from side to side as the wheels bumped and juddered under the strain. There were no other vehicles about. It was easy to see why the robbers had picked this stretch of road. Traffic couldn't move at more than a crawl. If it came to a chase it would have been quicker on foot. I kept scanning the undergrowth for signs of movement.

Now there was nothing on the car radio, none of the channels extended this far west. There were no telephones either. The telegraph poles were in place, but no lines were strung between them. There was scarcely any postal service either. People in Western Uganda who wished to communicate with those in the East gave their letters to the pick-up drivers and hoped they got through.

'How are you feeling?' asked Edward.

It was not a time for honesty. On the other hand, I didn't think I could carry off flagrant dishonesty either.

'Mildly apprehensive,' I said.

I couldn't stop thinking about grenades. Grenades and war comics. I had read these assiduously as a child. One in particular had always stuck with me. It followed a group of RAF volunteers as they trained to become bomber pilots. After a few weeks of this, the time came for them to fly their first mission over Germany. There was a man called Ralph who found it difficult to fit in with the rest of the crew. Everyone else was laughing and playing cards waiting for the signal to take off, but Ralph wasn't up to this. He was scared. Thought bubbles – always with broken or serrated edges as opposed to the unbroken lines that encircled speech – rose from his head expressing all kinds of doubts and fears. 'Look at all the other chaps. They're all so relaxed and casual while I'm tortured with worry. Everyone must realise it, but there's nothing I can do.'

The siren sounds. Ralph straps himself in. He hasn't said a word to anybody. The Lancasters climb up into the night sky and set off for Germany. The mission proves to be a great success – numerous munitions factories blown off the map, German war effort set back months, any casualties confined to the minor characters.

Back at the base spirits are high. There's a party in the officers' mess. Ralph is hovering uneasily on the fringes of the festivities when one of the other crew members comes up to him. 'I just want you to know how impressed we all were with your conduct before we took off tonight,' he says. 'I don't mind admitting now that the rest of us were scared stiff. We all sat around desperately trying to be cheerful, but inside we were shaking like leaves. But you were so cool and detached about everything. You were an example to us all.'

What ruined the story for me was that Ralph then confessed that he'd been just as frightened as everyone else. (If he'd had any sense he would have kept his mouth shut.) The moral being that you shouldn't judge people solely by their outward behaviour. But what happened to those who couldn't dissemble, I wondered? The ones who went hysterically and publicly to pieces. I saw myself in the same circumstances being dragged to the cockpit thrashing about in my flying suit, protesting vigorously, 'No, not me. There's been a terrible mistake. I really do want to fly a desk.'

The landscape was changing once more. The road still looked like collapsed mineworkings, but the countryside around had flattened out. Long-horned cattle grazed in fields bounded by high hedges. The heat haze seemed to corrugate the air. Trees quivered as if they were being shaken from below. Edward was explaining to Moses how one of his closest childhood friends was now working as an Exocet Missile salesman. I waited for five minutes and said, 'Do you think we're past the point where the robbers were?'

Edward turned round. He looked surprised. 'Oh yes,' he said. 'We passed that ages ago. Were you worried?'

'Worried?' I said it again, this time getting what I hoped was just the right note of affront into my voice. 'Worried?'

'No,' I said. 'Not worried. Just curious.'

A line of boys in combat uniform were running along the road two abreast. There was an officer bringing up the rear of the crocodile, trying without much success to keep them in step. The boys lolloped along, talking to one another, calling out to passers-by. These were the Kadogos, boy-soldiers from the guerilla war. Most were orphans whose parents had been killed by the then government troops. They had run away to the bush and joined up. Some were as young as seven or eight. In the bush they were given uniforms, weapons training and formed into brigades.

It was widely held that they had proved to be one of the guerillas' most valuable assets. They were loyal, brave and, above all, eager. But now the war was over they were a problem. No one knew what to do with them. The government had decided that it would institute an education programme whereby the Kadogos would go back to school and make up on the studies they had missed during the years of fighting.

The trouble was that the Kadogos didn't want to go back to school. After life in the trenches, the classroom seemed a very dull alternative. Several had escaped from the special Kadogo school in Mbarara. A few had turned to stealing, living in derelict buildings and holding up shops. They were supposed to have turned in their guns, but since there had never been a proper inventory of weapons given out in the first place, no one knew what percentage of them had been returned.

Most, however, went back to their old army commanders. The commanders were supposed to send them straight back to school. Few did. They kept them on as unofficial bodyguards, batmen and companions for their own children. Not that the Kadogos were likely to have much in common with anyone else their own age who hadn't served in the war. Many were now in their early teens, but they looked as if age had long since ceased to mean anything. You'd see them riding on the back of army Landrovers, legs over the sides, leaning into the breeze, rifles dangling from their shoulders.

Even out of uniform you could tell them apart from other children. It wasn't so much their manner, though this too was distinctive – an uneasy mix of swagger and suspicion – but their expressions. There was a weariness about them, a look that suggested they had lost for ever the capacity to be shocked by anything. This was what happened to real boy adventurers, given guns, a cause and the opportunity for heroics. They ended up unwanted and dead behind the eyes.

We went to deliver salt to one of Moses' sisters. A track led up between tiny windowless houses, some made of breeze blocks, others of mud. Moses' sister lived in a new house with a little wooden

94

stockade around it. Lines of washing were stretched between the fence posts. She came out to greet us, carrying a baby on her shoulder. The baby couldn't have been more than a few weeks old. Two other small children came out with her. When she moved the baby to shake our hands, I could see that she too had two dark matt patches of skin on one side of her neck.

It was lunchtime in Mbarara. On the main street shoppers swarmed round the market. The women, imperturbable, carrying bags of groceries on their heads. The men, as usual, a good deal less self-possessed. I could hear footsteps behind me. Then a hand landed on my shoulder. A man was standing there, small and fat in a belted, powder-blue safari suit. He looked terrifically pleased to see me. So much so that he simply stood and beamed for a while. I assumed he had mistaken me for someone else and was about to point this out when he said, 'You are English aren't you?'

I said I was. He looked even more pleased at this. 'My name is George,' he said. 'Forgive me for stopping you, but I thought how nice it would be for us to have a chat. I saw you walking down the street and I thought, I am right in the mood for a conversation.'

This was ominous. Easy banter with strangers has never been one of my strong points. Edward and Moses were off buying spark plugs for the pick-up. It was with a marked lack of grace that I said, 'What do you want to talk about?'

'I am starved of conversation,' he said. 'Quite starved. I can't tell you what pleasure it gives me to talk about England. The Weald of Kent. The Hog's Back. Those magnificent Seven Sisters culminating in that great lovers' leap, Beachy Head. It is not that I pine for England, you understand. Simply that I find descriptions of the English landscape so uplifting.

'You will, I'm sure, be familiar with the About Britain series of books edited by Geoffrey Grigson and published in the 1930s. Excellent books. Unfortunately, I have only the one on the Home Counties, but it is most enjoyable. Tell me, do you think Welwyn Garden City can be counted an absolute success in planning terms?'

He was, he said, a film producer. 'Most people don't even realise that there is a film industry in Uganda. Do you know why? Because no one ever makes any films. There is no money. The technical equipment keeps getting stolen and most of the cinemas have been blown up.'

I asked him when he had last made a film.

'Ah,' he said. 'Now, I think it was in 1974.'

Between films he had worked for the Ministry of Information in Kampala. There he had recruited Major Bob Astles, the retired English army officer who went on to become one of Idi Amin's closest cronies. This, he said, was one of the great mistakes of his life. Something that had been causing him recurrent spasms of guilt ever since.

'My God, what an idiot that man was,' he said. 'An idiot from the neck down. And a complete idiot from the neck up.'

A car was travelling very fast down the main road towards the market. There was a plume of black exhaust trailing out behind it and the roar of the engine sent pedestrians scuttling for cover. 'That fellow is going much too fast,' said George.

Just as he was about to pass us, the driver swung suddenly to the left, presumably intent on going through the two concrete pillars into the market. He was never going to make it. The car slammed into one of the pillars. The windscreen smashed and the engine hic-coughed and died. An angry crowd gathered round the car banging on the roof and what was left of the bonnet. The driver was dragged out. People started cuffing him around the ears and accusing him of driving like a maniac. He put his hands over his head to shield himself from the blows.

'Look at that,' cried George. 'Did you see? That's Uganda for you. Absolutely typical. He failed to negotiate. He completely failed to negotiate. Dear, oh dear, oh dear, oh dear.'

Eight

We drove on through the afternoon. The road dropped slowly down
into the western arm of the Rift Valley. There were villages hidden
among the trees and children selling cooked bananas by the side of
the road. Moses pulled hard on the wheel as we swung round the
side of a lake overhung with trees and elephant grass. The water
looked dark, the surface was quite still.

'That is a famous lake,' said Moses. 'It has no bottom.'

'No bottom at all?'

'Absolutely none.'

This was more like it. I preferred my lakes to be bottomless,
unfettered by measurements or practicality, to plunge straight to the
centre of the Earth in huge subterranean chutes.

Moses heaved on the wheel again and shoved the gearstick
forward. The road dipped sharply into a series of looping hair-pin
bends. The brakes squealed and the baggage slewed around in the
back. Moses was laughing to himself as the pick-up gathered speed.

All at once we broke through the trees and saw the floor of the
Rift Valley spread out in front of us, a great sweep of pale green
grass disappearing off into the mist. Through the clouds on the
horizon it was just possible to make out a grey, undulating smudge
that grew steadily darker as it climbed upwards. I already had my
arm raised and my mouth half open when Moses said, 'Yes. You see?
There they are. The mountains are not so far away.'

The pick-up rattled over the Bailey Bridge, a spray of gravel dropped
into the water below. In the middle of the bridge was a metal plaque
saying that it had originally been put up over the Thames during the
War, and then re-erected here in 1954, across the narrow channel
that divided Lake Edward from Lake George. The plaque was

crumbling away, a thick ridge of rust framed it round the outside. Dark brown rivulets ran down through the lettering.

On the far side of the bridge was another roadblock, a pole suspended over the road with a piece of sacking hanging off one end. The roadblocks had become like staging posts, little vetting stations you had to pass through before being admitted from one level to the next. The soldiers looked more disinterested than ever. Hardly any vehicles passed through here. Those that did were kept waiting while the soldiers finished their game of cards.

One of them lurched over. He had flat feet and his green Wellington boots were trodden down at the sides. He squatted down and held on to the window frame of the truck as he peered inside. There was a blast of thickly alcoholic breath. Moses gave a whinny of disapproval and reared back in his seat. The soldier's eyeballs swam around as he tried to get us all into focus. When he got up to wave us on he toppled to one side and had to grab on to the wing mirror to keep his balance.

One end of the pole was weighted, the soldier tripped again and fell on it. The other end shot into the air. You could hear it twanging, like elastic. As we drove underneath Moses said, despairingly, 'They have abandoned self-control.'

Stanley had passed this way in 1885, shortly after confirming that the mountains now massing along the horizon in the dusk were indeed the Mountains of the Moon. Lieutenant Stairs had made his brief exploration of the mountains two weeks earlier, but this was the first time that anyone in Stanley's party had got a good view of the whole range. Stanley described the moment with his usual blend of fulsomeness and rigorous attention to detail:

> The great mountain suddenly cast off its cloudy garments to gratify us once more. In rank after rank the mountainous ridges rose until Ruwenzori was revealed from end to end. From the south it looks like a range of about thirty miles in length with as many blunt-topped peaks, separated from each other by deep hollows. Up to this time we had estimated the height to be about 17,000 feet, but the revelation of the southern face, shrouded

with far-descending fields of deep and pure snow exalted it 1500 feet in the general opinion. I seized this opportunity to photograph the scene, that others might view the most characteristic image of Ruwenzori.

Stanley pitched camp on the shore of the lake and went out in a punt to take soundings – sediment was one of his special interests. 'The pole drops through four or five feet of grey mud to which are attracted thousands of minute mica flakes, fish scales and pulverised bones of fish which emit an overpowering stench.'

Nearby Stanley found the Little Salt Lake at Katwe. A place, he noted, of 'singularly dead and lonely appearance'. On reaching the shore of the Salt Lake, he was surprised to see that the water was blood red. There were deposits of some sort floating around in it: 'On looking down I found that this deposit floated like congealed blood on and below the surface.' All around him hundreds of butterflies lay dead on the sand. The salt had dried on their wings leaving them too heavy to get airborne.

He was not the first European to come here. Sir Samuel Baker had beaten him to it, arriving fifteen years earlier. Still, there were compensations for Stanley. He was spared from having to name anything – Baker, believing there was only one lake instead of two, had christened it Lake Albert Edward. Finding suitable names for geographical landmarks was to become an increasingly awkward business. By the time Stanley came along there was scarcely a member of the Royal Family who hadn't had a lake or mountain range in Africa named after them. Whereas once the choice had been straightforward enough, now the discovery of anything significant entailed some desperate trawling down among the deadbeats.

It was not until twenty years after Stanley's visit that there were found to be two lakes and they were rechristened Lake George and Lake Edward – a new generation of royal babies had been born by then, thus easing the pressure. But that wasn't the end of it. When Idi Amin took over in 1971 he decided that all such colonial relics would have to go. Renaming things was a major priority. Amin had very definite ideas about this. He wanted names that would banish all memories of colonial occupation and at the same time remind the local population of who was now boss. With characteristic immodesty he renamed Lake Edward Lake Idi Amin Dada. (By mutual agreement President Mobutu of Zaire, also keen on leaving his mark on the landscape, got to rename Lake Albert (to the north) Lake Mobutu.

But Lake George posed definite problems. Amin was stumped. There was just no other name he could think of that would do the trick. No one else was worthy of having a lake named after them, and he could hardly have another one of his own, quite so close by. So Lake George stayed as it was.

With the fall of Amin had come another crisis. Now he too had to be expunged from the map. But by then no one was too sure what the lakes had originally been called before Baker came. Besides, there were no facilities for printing new maps and so there was little point in renaming things. For the time being Lake Idi Amin Dada had reverted back to being called Lake Edward until someone worked out what to do.

The road curved round so that the mountains now rose in dark silhouette to our left. No features were visible, only a sense of vast bulk materialising alongside. There were bushbuck grazing in the savannah by the side of the road. These, though, were unlike any bushbuck I had ever seen. They didn't dart away like shoals of fish at the first sign of movement. Instead, they stumped off angrily to the nearest clump of bushes. They walked with stiff arthritic movements, their legs were dotted with sores. Even their skin looked faded. Later it turned out that all their predators had died out, hunted into extinction. Life had become an unfamiliar drift into old age. It didn't seem to agree with them. They had the glazed purposelessness of zoo animals with nothing left to fear.

Moses had the headlights on. He was urging the pick-up on through the fading light, sweettalking it one moment, berating it the next. A flock of cranes was flying overhead. You could hear as much as see them. The swish of wings and a dry gurgling sound as they called to one another.

Once I had been a master of out-of-body experiences. I roamed around the animal kingdom, up among the birds, squeezing in behind the sensory apparatus and taking over the controls for a while. It was simple enough. There was nothing to it. I was ten years old, lying in bed one night, when I woke to find myself hovering two feet above the bed, staring down at my sleeping form. This was a big surprise, no question of that, and to begin with I did nothing apart from try to work out which of us looked the more familiar. It was difficult, there was a general lack of substantiality about.

After a while, though, I began to feel less fearful. It might be unusual – no one I knew had ever been through anything like *this* before – it might not be the sort of thing to bring up in early conversation with strangers, but looked at collectedly it had distinct possibilities. This, after all, was only the start. Leaving your own body seemed easy enough. Getting into other ones was where the real challenge lay. Everything depended on picking just the right target. Before long the beasts and I had come to an understanding. They allowed me to saunter under their skins, while I – it was a reciprocal thing – had to put up with their encroachments. This was the less pleasant part. At night especially, I could feel them marauding around my insides, taking me over. Wild creatures – not just under the same blankets, but right there, wedged in your system. Even so, it was worth it. I saw the world through a whole host of different eyes. It was the greatest cure for boredom I had ever come across. After a while, as far as I was concerned, time spent on two legs was wasted time. I hankered after something more zoological.

A small crate arrived one day, brought by a man in a van with a wire mesh over the back windows. A note was attached to the crate, written in carefully looped handwriting, saying that the occupant was thought to be male. I levered off the top. There was a moist, faintly metallic smell that seemed to have come from a long way underground. Inside the crate was a tortoise lying on top of a mound of straw, scything its legs around. Beside it was a greenish puddle where it had been sick during the journey. I called the tortoise Charles after the Prince of Wales, for whom my admiration was tempered only by twinges of annoyance that he and not I had been marked out for eventual kingship.

The tortoise offered all kinds of opportunities for me to boost my new empathy with animals. And also to put even more ground between myself and those couples who could be seen careering around children's television in bush hats and Landrovers, sidling up to the wildlife and repeating the same wretched joke about shooting animals with cameras instead of guns. These people had no idea. For them it was just scientific. For me it was something far more special. It was personal.

I spent hours engaged in prolonged eye contact with Charles while I tried to imagine what it must be like to be a tortoise. All my energies were directed to relating to life inside a shell. And after several weeks I felt we were getting somewhere. An understanding was taking shape.

Or so I thought. One morning I settled down for another free exchange of impressions to find that Charles had disappeared. He had escaped. I went out looking for him, wondering what had gone wrong. Perhaps all this one-to-one stuff had got too much for him. I had been invading his space. All that day and the next I scoured the garden, without success. At the end of the second day I gave up looking.

It wasn't long before I forgot all about Charles. He had let me down, betrayed a trust. Then, a few weeks later, I was walking along the top of the field behind our house, up beyond the pigsty where I seldom went. There cradled between two molehills was Charles. I could see the C painted on his shell, showing through the long grass. I fell to my knees delighted – the recriminations could wait until later. I picked him up and as I did so, something long and white slithered out on to the ground. It looked like an early prototype for a frog.

It took me some moments to realise that this was Charles. His eyes were still open, turned upwards in an expression of terrible exasper-ation. But around his extremities he had begun to flake away, little coils of decaying skin lay scattered around where he had fallen, while in the middle of his back his body had jellified, become almost transparent. I shrank away in horror. This had all sorts of implications. For a start he was a long way from the house. In tortoise terms this was an epic trek. There was only one possible explanation. He must have really wanted to get away from me. I'd come on too strong, been altogether too intense.

From then on things were never quite the same. There was no longer any glimmer of recognition when I caught the eye of another species. We gazed at one another implacably. There was nothing between us, nothing at all.

Soon after that, the Royal Family and I began to drift apart too. For years afterwards, whenever I saw Prince Charles on television I could never quite shake off the conviction that he was an impostor and the real heir to the throne had rotted away inside his shell, alone at the top of our field with only me to witness the consequences. What a thing to happen. The Romanovs thought they had come off badly, this surely was far worse.

But the final parting of the ways didn't come until a number of years later. I was by myself in Trafalgar Square late one night not feeling at all well. I had drunk one and a half bottles of a cough mixture widely credited with having hallucinogenic properties. I had finished the first bottle without much difficulty, washing it down with lemonade. Having bought two bottles – I had feigned chronic bronchitis for the benefit of the chemist, so successfully I could scarcely croak out my order – it seemed a shame to leave the other one completely unbroached. On the other hand, drinking two bottles might well have been overdoing it. I compromised by taking a few sips from the second bottle and leaving it at that. I thought of it as a kind of chaser.

Nothing much happened for a while. And then my whole metabolism began to grind to a halt. Everything just got slower and slower. My heart appeared to beat about once a minute. My pulse had disappeared completely – I ran my hands up and down my arms trying to find where it had gone. There seemed a distinct possibility that I might be clinically dead. The slightest movement was an enormous strain. Walking, it felt as if the paving stones had stuck to my feet.

I sat on the base of one of Landseer's lions and tried to work out what to do. The last Tube had gone and there were no night buses about. I set off to walk home, and had struggled to the side of the road when a large black Rolls Royce drew up at the traffic lights alongside.

Behind the smoked glass I could see the Queen staring at me. My first reaction was one of enormous relief. I'd always felt that the Queen had a certain responsibility for me. More recognisably there than God, less fearsome than Ayesha, she represented a kind of indiscriminate benevolence that offered crumbs of comfort in an emergency. I felt that this debt should not go unacknowledged. Holding on to the lamppost with one hand, I raised the other and waved. It was a kind of slow, arcing wave, like a hypnotist's watch swinging on a surprisingly steady axis.

But as I waved I realised that I was doing something wrong. I had appropriated the Queen's one big gesture for myself. The only possible channel of communication between us had opened the wrong way. Her expression did not change. Behind the smoked glass, she continued to regard me with complete indifference. Then the lights changed to green and the Rolls Royce pulled away, turning through Admiralty Arch and speeding off down the Mall.

My out-of-body experiences dropped right off. Now I was stuck with what I'd got, the scope for excursions massively curtailed. But just occasionally I felt the tug that signalled a brief spell of separation, a fleeting taste of what had been. It happened now as I sat behind Moses watching an ant walk round the rim of his sun-hat. I thought of Charles leaving his shell and nose-diving on to the grass. It wasn't quite the same thing, but there seemed to be certain similarities as I rose to join the cranes, looking down on a dark roaring shape pushing a pool of light before it through the darkness. Hardly scorching a distinctive furrow across the map. But even so, the only thing for miles around worth following, and good from this angle.

The Margherita Hotel stood on top of a hill outside Kasese. The drive ran between flowerbeds that had long since grown over to a porch strung with coloured light bulbs. Turquoise paint hung in peeling strips from the walls, cracked and brittle like old stamp hinges.

Moses insisted on staying with the pick-up. He was planning to sleep behind the wheel in case anyone decided to steal our drum of petrol. Edward and I tried to persuade him to come inside. He shook his head. 'Thieves will come,' he said.

'Surely not here,' we argued. 'There's no one around.'

Moses was unconvinced. 'Temptation . . .' He shrugged and looked down the drive to a group of huts where torch-beams played about in the darkness. 'I must wait,' he said.

Fires were burning on the hills. A ring of orange beacons encircled us, great showers of sparks rose into the night. Stepping down from the pick-up I could think of only one thing. 'It's a sign,' I thought. 'It has to be a sign.' And then, worse still, 'They must know I'm coming.' I grabbed hold of Edward's sleeve. 'Look,' I said – my voice had thickened into a kind of precognitive wheeze – 'Look at the fires.'

'They're burning grass,' said Edward.

'Grass?' I wanted to say. 'It may be grass to you, but it looks very much like a portent to me.' I kept quiet, though. You had to be careful. Being susceptible to such things pointed reliably towards a loosening hold on reality. Talking about them removed any possible doubts.

We went inside to register. Hanging on the wall by the reception desk was a large black-and-white aerial photograph of the Mountains of the Moon with the main peaks labelled: Stanley, Baker, Stairs, etc. Faint dotted trails ran along the ridges to the summits showing the routes taken by the first climbers. In the top left-hand corner was a dark smudge where the wing-tip of the plane had got in the way.

The woman behind the desk was reading a magazine. She looked up in surprise as we walked in. Surprise turned to consternation when we said we wanted to stay. She pulled out the register and leafed through the pages, frowning at the entries and clicking her tongue.

'You must have rooms,' said Edward.

'Rooms with facilities?' she asked.

'What sort of facilities?'

The woman looked even more unhappy. 'Beds?'

She took a key from a row of hooks beside the desk. There was no number 13. Instead she reached for 12A.

'Do you have another number?' I asked.

'You are superstitious?'

'He is a primitive mzungu,' explained Edward. The woman laughed. She looked at me with a sympathetic tilt of her head. I couldn't help it. I was superstitious. 12A didn't fool me. Numerologically it was still a trouble spot.

'I think you'll find 12A is the best we have to offer,' she said. 'Better facilities.'

'We'll take it,' said Edward.

A man in a white linen jacket came to take our bags. The floor was made of black asphalt. There were patches of dried glue where the carpet tiles had been torn up. The previous manager had been arrested and charged with theft. In the absence of guests, he was believed to have sold much of his furniture to pay himself and the staff.

We walked down a long corridor. Pink doors opened off on either side, some had chisel marks on the lintels. Twenty years before this had been one of the most elegant hotels in East Africa – along with the Mountains of the Moon Hotel in Fort Portal to the north, whose telegraphic address had simply been 'Romance'. People came here to walk in the foothills, to climb, to play golf on the hotel's own course and take safaris into the bush. But now scarcely anyone came. The grass on the golf course was waist high in places and most of the animals had disappeared.

There was a copper mine up the road that had once provided work for much of the local population. The whole area was rich in copper so at least the raw material had been there for Idrisi's Dome. But the mine had ceased production in the early 1970s when the price of copper fell. Ever since then close on a thousand men had turned up, unpaid, every day to carry out repair work and ensure that the mine was set to recommence production at a moment's notice. Occasionally people – mostly westerners but latterly a few Japanese

– would come to have a look round and talk of getting the mine opened again. The talk, however, never came to anything and the mine stayed out of action.

'It's ridiculous to be so superstitious,' said Edward as we followed the porter's white jacket down a stretch of corridor, unlit except for a single bulb of the lowest wattage imaginable set high into the ceiling.

'It's not necessarily a sign of stupidity,' I said. 'Joyce was very superstitious.'

'Joyce who?'

'James Joyce. There's a story about his going out into a street in Paris one night and inviting a complete stranger to have dinner with him because he didn't want to sit down at a table with twelve other people.'

'Why not?'

'Because it's unlucky. Look at the precedents. Look at Jesus.'

'Unlucky?' said Edward, stopping. 'That wasn't bad luck. That was predestination.'

The porter too had stopped. It was just possible to make out the letters 12A on the door in front of us. He fumbled in his pocket for the key, turned it in the lock and then reached inside to flick a switch. There was a faint fizzing noise just before the lights came on. Two single beds covered in yellow candlewick bedspreads were set either side of what looked like a tin trunk.

'If you want hot water then you must call me,' said the porter. 'I'm afraid it no longer comes out of the taps. But we can boil saucepans in the kitchen and bring you the water in buckets.' As he was about to leave he stuck his head back round the door and said, 'I almost forgot. Dinner is served.'

In the bar a bat flew over the billiard table, quite bare of green baize except for a few tufts that still hung around the pockets. On one side of the bar there was a mural showing various animals, mainly hippos and gorillas, lined up as if for a school photograph with the mountains behind them. Blotched with mould, they gazed glumly out from the wall.

We were the only guests in the dining room. Five waiters, also in white linen jackets, were standing behind a long buffet table. There were two pineapples on either end of the table and a pile of cutlery in the middle. One of the waiters came with the menu. He bent forward to hand it to us, legs quite straight, one arm crooked behind his back.

The first course was a choice between bread and butter and soup, the second beef or tilapia fish.

'What would you recommend?' asked Edward.

'I would not advise the beef,' he said.

'Tough?'

'I'm afraid so.' He paused, his mouth half open. Not exactly a smile, it suggested the memory of something stuck between his teeth. He lowered his voice. 'And rather fatty.'

The soup was tasteless and heavy with cornflour. It shrank away from the sides of the plate and bulged towards the centre. Three of the waiters remained standing behind the buffet table while the other two went through swing doors into the kitchen. The bat flew in from the bar and swooped over the empty tables.

We had just finished our soup when all the lights went out. There were cries from the kitchen, more of disappointment than annoyance. White shapes began to move around the dining room, whispering to one another. A match was struck, a gas lamp lit and one of the waiters carried it over. He took away a jug of flowers and set down the lamp, roaring, in the middle of the table.

'Do you get many power cuts?' I asked.

'Many power cuts,' he repeated. 'They say that the head of the power station has walked off with the electricity revenue. He has been eating.'

Eating was the – highly apt – Ugandan phrase for corruption. You heard it all the time. So and so has been eating, usually very well. More rarely, he has been caught eating. Everyone seemed to be at it. 'We are an eating economy,' I had heard a university lecturer say sadly, back in Kampala. The District Administrators were known to be particularly bad offenders. One sure sign that they had been 'eating' was when they blew an enormous amount on their daughters' weddings.

'Can it be Mr Cathcart?' said a voice close by, from the darkness.

'It can,' said Edward.

A man stepped forward out of the shadows. 'Ngugi,' he said. 'Remember me, Ngugi of the Fairview. I said to myself, that is Mr Cathcart. I was quite sure of it.' He was the manager. Prior to coming here, it turned out, he had managed the hotel in Kampala where Edward had stayed when he first came to Uganda.

He had taken over the hotel in Kampala at an awkward time. The previous manager had left in unusual circumstances. Angry at not having been paid for several weeks, the staff had demanded a meeting with him and the chief accountant. The meeting took place in the manager's office on the ground floor. Tempers soon frayed. Realising that things were going badly, the manager and the chief accountant jumped through the window and made off down the street. The enraged staff piled out after them. The accountant was caught and beaten up on one of the main roundabouts in Kampala, but the manager was never seen again. Mr Ngugi had been appointed in his place.

Now he had been transferred here. It could hardly have been any kind of promotion. He asked if he could sit down and lowered himself into a chair with an air of great weariness, almost despair. There was a handkerchief spilling out of the breast pocket of his jacket. He pulled it out and began mopping his brow.

'What did you think of the soup?' he asked.

'Floury,' said Edward. 'Very floury.'

'I know,' said Mr Ngugi. 'You're quite right. Packet soups are not what they were.'

'But why doesn't the hotel make soup?' said Edward. 'Uganda is one of the most fertile countries in the world. Look at all the vegetables that are grown. Surely it wouldn't be too difficult.'

Mr Ngugi gave no indication of having heard. He seemed sunk into a melancholy stupor. Eventually he said, 'The liquidiser has disappeared. Besides, people round here prefer a brand name.'

'I will be frank with you,' he said after another long pause. 'We have more packet soup than we know what to do with. My predecessor must have done a deal with someone – he was a rather bad sort I'm afraid, a plentiful eater. There are boxes of the stuff out the back. We have enough soup here to last us well into the next century.' He looked at our plates – the remains of the soup was already crusting around the rim. 'What flavour did you have?'

'It said asparagus on the menu,' said Edward.

'Yes, that's right, asparagus,' said Mr Ngugi. 'Of course, I typed it myself. The pea is a deeper green.'

The lights came back on for a few seconds and then went out again. Mr Ngugi behaved as if nothing unusual had happened. 'I look back on my days in Kampala with great happiness,' he said. 'There were entire weeks when we were fully booked. But here, I'm afraid, it's an altogether different story. There is no passing trade, you see. Not a thing. A couple stayed here last week, from Belgium. They complained about the accommodation. I said to them, it is difficult to be a hotelier with honour in Uganda these days. We are doing our best in difficult circumstances.'

He got up to go. The lights came back on. We waited, motionless, for them to go off again, but this time they stayed on. 'What did you order to follow?' he asked.

'Tilapia fish,' we said.

Mr Ngugi nodded approvingly. 'A good choice.' He went off into the kitchen nearly colliding in the swing doors with the waiter bringing our main course.

The tilapia fish was set down on the table with great care. We had one each. Mine lay sprawled across the plate, its mouth gaping open as if it was making one last lunge for the pile of mashed potato just out of reach. It was excellent, like mullet, with translucent bones as broad as the prongs on my fork.

As we finished eating the power began to fade again, not disappearing completely this time but dimming so much that the filaments in the bulbs were no brighter than matchheads on the point of burning out. We got up and felt our way out of the dining room and up the long darkened corridor to our room. The beds had been turned down, the folds in the sheets standing out sharp and white against the gloom.

I got into bed and fell immediately into a deep sleep, quite dreamless apart from one brief moment when I saw – or thought I saw – Ursula Andress as pale and translucent as the bones of the tilapia fish. She was standing on an outcrop of rock surrounded by dark green trees and waving her hands in front of her face. I couldn't work out if she was beckoning or just swatting away some flies.

The next morning I woke up early and went outside on to the hotel terrace. The sun was just coming up. All around the mountains were pink in the morning light. Mist rolled down the slopes. There were a few thin trails of smoke and blackened patches where the fires had been the night before. Long green ridges like fingers rose from the valley floor and stretched out towards one another, climbing into the cloud. There was dew on the grass that sparkled as the sun hit it.

I felt extraordinarily lightheaded. It was as if I were gazing through a screen of gauze. Nothing stayed quite in focus. The whole landscape looked soft, rubbery, as if it had just been moulded into shape and was still waiting for a few extra imprints. I hung on to the handrail and thought about what mysteries had lain hidden in the mountains for so long, what dreams had found a home here. The primal fountains, the great Dome of Idrisi, the eighty-five copper statues. Then, of course, there were my own dreams, every bit as wild and unlikely. But now I had actually arrived I found I could hardly recall them, could only just conjure up the flash of a disappearing tutu as another childhood hero flounced off into extinction.

One of the maids was sweeping the terrace, coming towards me wielding her broom in front of her in broad rasping strokes. Dust dropped off the terrace and settled on the flowerbeds below.

At breakfast the same five waiters were lined up behind the buffet table in their linen jackets. They could have been there all night. When we came in they lent forward together in a rheumatoid stage bow.

We ordered toast and coffee. When they arrived I asked the waiter if there was any marmalade. He giggled and took a step back as if I'd just suggested something improper. 'Marmalade?' he said. He wiped his face with the back of his hand to cover his embarrassment. 'I don't think so, sir. I will go and look.'

There were shouts of laughter from the kitchen. A few minutes later the waiter came back. He looked part bemused, part affronted, as though he had just cottoned on to being the butt of a practical joke. 'You will find no marmalade here,' he said.

Moses came in. He had showered and changed. Drops of water stood up on top of his head and quivered when he moved. He did not look at all pleased. His shoulders were sloped, his mouth downturned. 'Well,' we asked. 'Did anyone try and steal our petrol?'

'No,' he said. 'They did not.'

Something had gone wrong. The thieves had not appeared. Moses toyed with a piece of toast, haunted by the possibility that he may have been hoodwinked or outwitted. When the waiter came to ask him what he wanted – I noticed that he gave me a wide berth, walking in a hurried nervous way around the back of my chair – Moses shook his head and waved him away.

In order to go walking in the mountains you had first to hire porters. There was only one man in the area empowered to provide porters and he lived several miles away, up an unmarked track that led from the main road into the hills. We would have to find him, tell him what we were planning to do and buy the right supplies – there was a stipulated amount of food and equipment per porter. There was also a special mountain licence that had to be obtained from the District Administrator's office. Depending on whether the right people were around and there was no hold-up with the licence, this could take anything between a day and a week.

The pick-up bumped up a gravel track, past a school where the children sat out on the grass in a semi-circle. They chanted out responses while the teacher pointed at questions on a blackboard set against a tree. The track grew narrower, twisting back on itself as it climbed the hillside. After a few miles of this we saw an elderly man standing in the middle of the road ahead, holding a large forked stick. As we drew nearer he raised his stick and held it up in front of him. He was wearing a long white shirt that reached almost to his knees.

'That man looks like he's walked out of the Old Testament,' said Edward.

The resemblance had not escaped Moses who had already embarked on a series of sharp intakes of breath.

112

First the fires, now this. It was like being under some kind of scriptural bombardment. When we got closer I could see that the man had a canvas shopping bag hanging from the fork of his stick. The pick-up came to a halt a couple of feet away from where he was standing.

'What are you searching for?' he asked. He had a low, sonorous sort of voice.

'Oh no. Really. Toot the horn and get him to go away.'

However, the man clearly had no intention of budging. He stood in the road, glaring at the radiator grille, his stick held firmly beside him. Up close he was surprisingly small, with a narrow strip of closely cropped moustache. We told him that we were looking for the Ibanda Mountain Club and its agent John Matte. At this, he looked us over very deliberately, raking us up and down with a long unblinking gaze.

'Why are you looking for him?'

'We wish to go walking in the mountains.'

'I am Matte,' he said. 'I am the man you seek.'

He got into the pick-up alongside me, holding his stick between his knees. He said how fortunate we were to find him; he seldom walked down this road at this time of day. Today, though, he had to go into Kasese. Now we could give him a lift and he would show us where to buy provisions for the porters.

'When do you want to set out?' asked Matte. 'Tomorrow?'

'Don't you think tomorrow is a bit soon?' I said to Edward. 'We could rest up and get properly acclimatised.'

'Tomorrow?' said Edward. 'Tomorrow would be excellent.'

Moses turned the pick-up round and we bumped back down the track towards the road. I asked Matte why he was going to Kasese. 'It is a case of murder,' he said. A Swiss girl had been murdered nearby a few months earlier. Now two men had been arrested. Statements were being taken from anyone who had seen the girl. 'Lucky for you,' said Matte. 'You can get your mountain licence in the same place where I have to give my statement.'

The District Administrator's office was a long single-storey colonial building draped in bougainvillaea and surrounded by little circular prefab huts made of galvanised iron. We were shown into an office almost entirely wallpapered in 'Beware The Sweetness and Splendour of Sex' posters. A man sat behind a desk shuffling dockets into different trays.

'You want to go walking in the mountains, starting tomorrow?' He shook his head. 'It's not easy.'

'Why not?'

'It's not easy because it's unusual.'

He searched through a filing cabinet for the right set of forms, found what he was looking for and then realised that they had been superseded by another set of regulations. There was some doubt as to whether the new forms had in fact been issued. In the end he decided to use the original forms making various handwritten additions to correspond with what he thought were the new amendments. 'Of course,' he said as he handed us the papers, 'it's all bureaucracy. No one will ever ask you for the licence. The chances of meeting anyone up there – ' he nodded out of the window to where the hills rose sharply behind – 'are virtually non-existent.'

There was another form outlining the food and equipment we needed to buy for the porters. 'Shoes are not necessary except on snow,' it said. However, one blanket (cotton) had to be provided per man, to remain his property at the end of the trip. So too must pangas – again one per man – so they could hack a way through the undergrowth. As for food, the porters, it seemed, lived on an exclusive diet of cassava flour and smoked fish, with two cigarettes (Sportsman brand) to be given out to each man at the end of every day.

Outside it had begun to rain. It spattered down on the bougainvillaea and drummed on the roofs of the iron huts. Clerks ran from one hut to another with piles of papers on their heads wrapped in strips of cotton. As we were leaving the man said, 'Pity about the weather, eh?'

The rain grew even stronger. The paths turned to mud, the water cascaded down the gutters of the District Administrator's building with such force that it overshot the oil drums placed underneath to catch it. Edward and I sat in the pick-up with Moses waiting for

Matte to finish giving his statement. 'This is not good,' said Edward. 'This is very, very bad.'

Moses was reading a Christian journal which began its editorial with an attack on the man who had referred to anti-government rebels as biological substances and grabbed my lapels in the Sardinia Restaurant. 'We are all God's creatures,' it said. 'All equal in the sight of the Lord. This man is the victim of confused thinking. He would do well to study the Book of Genesis and walk once more down the paths of Righteousness.' Moses, who was saved already and knew this, seemed more interested in reading an article on 'Alcoholism and You'.

'Do you want to play Botticelli?' said Edward.

'What is it?'

'It's a word game. You pick a character, someone famous, and tell me what letter their surname begins with. I have to guess who they are, but you also have to guess who I think you are.'

'All right.'

'Who are you then?'

'I am H.'

I was looking over Moses' shoulder. 'What are you doing to yourself?' said the article. 'It's not too late. A lot of people do things under the influence of alcohol that they later regret. They fear that the Devil has got into them. And perhaps, in a way, they are right.'

'Did you live in Oxford and suggest a scientific explanation for the Star of Bethlehem?'

'No, I am not Halley.'

Moses was reading intently. 'Can we say that evil spirits reside within the bottle, that damnation lies at the bottom of a glass? Not necessarily. But remember that while a great many people think that there is no harm in a few social drinks to boost their confidence and make them feel more relaxed, their moral fabric is being eaten away. And one day you wake up and there is nothing left.'

'Are you the author of a book whose first sentence is "I get the willies when I see closed doors."?'

'No, I am not Joseph Heller.'

The rain was easing off, the view through the windscreen returning to normal. The man who had given us our mountain licences came out on to the verandah with a broom and brushed some puddles on to the grass. I could see Matte coming out of one of the iron huts and walking towards us, deep in conversation with another man.

'Are you by any chance the three-goal hero of England's World Cup victory over West Germany in 1966?'

'Yes,' I said. 'I am Geoff Hurst.'

The main street of Kasese consisted of two rows of one-storey buildings either side of a broad dirt road. A man with a rifle under his arm walked down the middle of the road stepping round the potholes that had filled up with rainwater. 'This is the Wild West of Uganda,' said Edward.

'Very wild,' agreed Moses.

But there was a battle going on for the soul of Kasese. On one side of the street, blasting out of the Paris Hotel, was Kenny Rogers singing, 'Ruby Don't Take Your Love to Town'. Directly opposite, a group of evangelists had set up their own sound equipment under an awning. They stood huddled in a little patch of shade singing along with 'Silent Night' as it strained through their speakers. 'They are saved,' said Moses, pointing at the evangelists. His finger switched to the other side of the street. 'And they are not.'

The occupants of the Paris Hotel looked to be some way from salvation. Several of them stood outside holding beer bottles and jeering at the evangelists while the volume was periodically cranked up inside to try and drown out the carol singing. But the evangelists appeared undeterred by this, redoubling their efforts each time the volume was increased. 'All is quiet. All is bright,' they bellowed.

Over the road the hotel speakers had distorted horribly as Kenny Rogers sang, 'It's hard to love a man whose legs are bent and paralysed.' Out in the sunlight, down on one knee, a man in a dark suit was exhorting the evangelists on. He looked like he was cheering a tug of war team. At the end of 'Silent Night' the evangelists launched straight into 'Oh Come All Ye Faithful.'

'Why are they singing Christmas carols?' I asked Moses. 'It's the middle of February.'

'They are strong songs,' he said.

The volume was being turned up still higher at the hotel. It looked for a while as though the evangelists had lost the battle. You could hardly hear them for Kenny Rogers. But all at once the hotel speakers went dead, either through mechanical failure or an attack of conscience on behalf of the owner. The evangelists, approaching the final crescendo of 'Oh come let us adore him', suddenly found they had the field to themselves and, now that volume was no longer the main priority, endeavoured to finish with some semblance of harmony.

As they finished there was a burst of applause from the Paris Hotel. Several more people had come out to see what was going on and they shouted what sounded like words of encouragement to the carol singers who stood under their awning, shifting awkwardly from side to side, not knowing quite what to make of this.

By the market two enormously fat women swathed in scarves were fanning one another. Matte had met up with a friend of his. Together, they said, they would buy everything we needed. All we had to do was give them the money. We peeled off some bills. Matte stuffed them in his pocket.

When Moses heard about this he assumed we were joking. As the realisation sunk in that we were telling the truth, he looked as if he had been winded and was struggling for air. 'Ugandan cheats,' he wheezed. And then, as if this was a lesson he had told us many times and should not need to repeat, 'They steal, steal, steal.' We explained that it had seemed best under the circumstances, but Moses was inconsolable. He sat in the pick-up, his fist against his cheek, as Matte and his friend dumped what appeared to be an endless succession of provisions into the back.

All the stalls in the market looked to be selling much the same things. There were piles of Lux soap – 'the soap used by International Film Stars', bottles of skin lighteners and sacks of powdered milk that were supposed to have been given away free as part of a UN aid programme, but had somehow been diverted on to the open market. They had a large red logo printed on the hessian with the words

'Food Aid' underneath. Men sat cross-legged on the ground meas-
uring plastic cupfuls on to sets of scales while people waited patiently
in line.

Skin lighteners had come back into fashion in Uganda after being
out of style for some years. This had upset doctors who complained
that they should be banned altogether. Not only did the lighteners
bleach the skin, they also made it very thin. When people had stitches
put in, their skin would just tear apart. No one could afford to cover
their whole body with cream. Most of them just put it on their faces,
with a dividing line around their necks that made it look as if their
heads had been transplanted on to different bodies.

At the Saad Hotel people crouched low over the Formica tables
and spoke in voices scarcely above a whisper. Whenever anyone came
in there was a momentary lull and then conversations would start up
again. This was where many of the smuggling schemes to and from
Zaire were hatched. But recently there had been a crack-down. The
army was more in evidence than before – dark green Landrovers
hurtled down the main street, Kadogos hanging over the sides – and
patrols along the border had been stepped up. Some of the smugglers
had taken to crossing the mountains on foot, but the more experi-
enced ones reckoned this was overdoing it – far too arduous, as well
as time-consuming.

A man came in and sat down at our table. He was white and
covered in bites. There was hardly an inch of him that hadn't come
up in angry red lesions. Even his ear lobes looked inflamed. He
couldn't stop scratching. His hands were constantly darting about
trying to quell a new outbreak of itching. 'I'm English,' he said,
dragging his fingernails down his forearms. 'I've just been up in the
mountains. Unbelievable. Just amazing.'

Unbelievable in what way, we asked. But he didn't want to be
specific. 'In every way. The whole thing. Incredible.' He looked
manic. His eyeballs bulged in a way that made you suspect pressure
round the back was reaching critical levels. He also had a very loud
voice. This was not in keeping with the general tone of the place.
People at neighbouring tables looked round in disapproval. He didn't
notice.

'Moss,' he said. 'Are you keen on moss?'

Edward and I looked at one another. 'Quite keen,' I said.

'There's a lot of it up there.' He laughed. It was more a startled bark than a laugh. 'Ha ha, yes, an awful lot of moss.'

He had ordered a cup of milky tea. When the waiter brought it he drank the tea from the spoon, like soup, flicking it from the cup into his mouth. Most of it ended up on the table, a brown puddle that spread rapidly towards the edges.

'How long were you up there?'

He shook his head. 'I can't remember. A week. Maybe two. You lose all track of time. I feel a different man, though, I don't mind telling you. The only trouble is I can't get rid of these bloody bites.' He held out his arms, nobbled with lumps, for closer inspection. 'One of the porters gave me some ointment. Didn't do any good at all. Turned out to be for fibrositis. Those insects really loved me, you know. They really loved me.' When he had finished his tea he got up, wished us goodbye, and walked out without paying. Neither of us said anything for a while.

Matte and his friend had finished shopping. The pick-up was piled high with sacks of food and cooking pots. The pangas lay on top. They looked like old cutlasses, their blades long and curved and already speckled with rust. We arranged to meet Matte the following morning. 'I will have the porters ready,' he said. 'You have nothing to fear.'

Moses drove us back to the Margherita in silence. The waiters were out by the staff quarters. They were wearing shorts and singlets and kicked a football about in the driveway. A woman was rinsing a tin plate under a tap.

The staff quarters were set to one side of the hotel, a line of tiny concrete boxes without windows. There was a row of breeze blocks inset with airholes round the top of each box. Inside the nearest one you could see two narrow bunk beds, one on top of the other, a plastic washing-up bowl and some clothes hanging from the corner of the top bunk.

The woman from reception brought two buckets of hot water to our room. She was smiling when she came in, but the muscles in her cheeks had tightened up with the strain of carrying the buckets. I sat in a few inches of dark lukewarm water and rubbed some more dirt into me with a flannel. Edward was standing by the window, looking down towards the golf course. There were pink and blue blossoms lying on the grass outside.

'Where do you think we'll be tomorrow night?' I asked.

'In the middle of fucking nowhere,' said Edward.

The lights went out before we had even started dinner. We picked our way down the corridor by torchlight. There were the five waiters standing behind the buffet table, lit from below by the gas lamp. Once again we were the only guests. The menu was the same as it had been the night before. But tonight a different waiter brought our tilapia fillets on a huge oval serving dish. The manager did not come over. He stood in the corner by the door to the bar with his hands clasped behind his back. It was tempting to imagine him dreaming of a throng of people at the dining tables, of elaborate menus, double-bookings and temperamental chefs in the kitchen.

That night all the lights came back on just as I had dropped off to sleep. We had left all the switches down and the room suddenly burst into light. I sat upright in bed, hands tightened round the sheet, trying to work out what was going on.

Nine

A sign was stuck into the ground. The letters burnt into the wood spelled out Ibanda Mountain Club with an arrow off to the right. But the sign had been knocked askew and the arrow now pointed almost vertically into the air, up towards the top of a clump of overhanging trees. About thirty men were standing outside a long low mud hut. They drew back as Moses drove up, lining the verge and watching in silence. When we got out the men craned forward for a better look.

Several naked children were playing in the dirt, their bodies caked with earth. Stiff, conical belly-buttons jutted from swollen stomachs. Matte came out – minus his forked stick this time – and brushed the children away. Most of them turned out to be his. He told the men to unload our bags. This was too much for Moses. He didn't like the idea of strangers touching the pick-up. As soon as anybody tried to lift one of our bags he rushed around to the tailgate and stood there, arms outstretched to fend them off. The men looked astonished. Whenever one of them took a tentative step forward Moses would flail his arms about and shout until they dropped back.

'Your friend,' said Matte, 'is behaving strangely.'

In the end a compromise was worked out whereby we handed our bags to the men who then set them down on the ground, holding each one up at arm's length before they did so, to test its weight.

Matte ushered us inside the hut. There was a wooden trestle table in the middle of the floor covered with coils of rope and a pile of crampons. It smelled like an old potting shed. On the back of the door someone had written in chalk, 'All Will Be Saved Now'. The writing was very tall and narrow, like violent fluctuations on a graph.

A man was leaning against the table. He wore lime green trousers and a yellow checked sports jacket and had a small goatee beard. Matte introduced us. This was Daniel, he would be our guide. Daniel smiled. One of his front teeth was missing, and when he stopped smiling his top lip got snagged in the gap. He smiled again to release it. Around his neck he had a gold cross on a chain.

'Now we will choose the porters,' said Matte. Outside, the men fell silent. Matte told them to get into line. They stood in a large semi-circle around the front of the hut. Most of them wore clothes that were in the final stages of disintegration. Sweaters unravelled round their chests, trousers threatened to shed legs. They were all from the Bakonjo tribe, famous both for their lack of size and their toughness. Although nothing like as small as the pygmies 50 miles to the north, they seldom scaled over 5 foot 3 inches. But their stamina was prodigious. Following a Bakonjo, it was said, was like following a motorcycle.

During colonial rule the British had found it difficult to enforce discipline in Bakonjo schools. It was decided that in future pupils should be caned if they misbehaved. The scheme was not a success. The Bakonjos took down their trousers and bent over obligingly enough, but the canes merely bounced off their buttocks. There was no sign of bruising afterwards, nor indeed any sign that they were in the slightest pain.

They were not, however, too keen on going up into the mountains. Part of this was superstition – they believed that evil spirits lived on the tops of the peaks; part mere disinclination – they couldn't understand why anyone would want to go up there. The only inducement was money and the daily rates were at least three times what they could hope to earn from farming. These worked out at the equivalent of 25 pence a day, with the rate to be doubled if it rained.

Daniel and Matte walked slowly down the line. Matte with his hands clasped behind his back and his chin out as if he was inspecting a guard of honour. Every so often, Daniel would reach out and touch someone on the shoulder. Those who had been picked were told to go and wait inside the hut. When the eight had been chosen the rest of the men drifted away, one or two of them kicking the earth with their bare feet in disappointment.

It turned out that Matte had miscalculated. There weren't enough provisions for eight men. One of them was sent off to the nearest village to see if he could buy some dried fish. The rest started to repack everything into old sacks. The sacks were then tied to harnesses of twisted banana leaves. These were strung round the porters' foreheads so that the sacks rested on their backs. Each porter could carry up to 22 kilos – a fully laden sack.

Inside the hut Matte opened a cupboard and pulled out a large leather-bound ledger. The pages had turned yellow and crinkled so badly at the front that the book appeared ready to burst open of its own accord. He pushed aside the pile of crampons to make space and sat down behind the table. An inkwell was brought and a fountain pen. Matte wrote down our names and those of the porters – most were known only by their Christian names. When he had finished, he picked up a pair of crampons with the end of his pen and swung them in front of us. We would, he explained, need to take a pair each if we were planning to go up beyond the snow-line.

'What do you think?' said Edward.

'Certainly not.'

'I don't know,' he said. 'I've always wanted to walk on African snow.'

'You're mad. You'll fall down a crevasse.'

'Not if we're roped together.'

'You won't be roped to me. I don't want anything to do with it.'

Edward couldn't make up his mind. In the end he decided that he would pick a pair of crampons and see if they fitted. They didn't. Matte offered another pair. These were no better. They needed adjustment. Moses went out to the pick-up and fetched the tool kit. A pair were loosened until they fitted over Edward's boots. He tied them on and stood up. The porters looked on in surprise as Edward tottered about, balanced uneasily on long metal spikes.

'How do they feel?'

'I'm not sure. How do they look?'

'They look odd.'

He embarked on a series of circuits of the inside of the hut. The crampons were inclined to get stuck in the mud floor making progress awkward. None the less he stuck to it doggedly. Children were pulled out of his path, porters flattened themselves against the walls.

Matte said, 'I've never seen anyone do that before.' There was an edge of something in his voice. It sounded almost like admiration. I asked if I might have a look at his ledger. He handed it to me, with some show of reluctance. The earliest entries were all but invisible, faint brown scratches and what looked like tiny drawings in the margin. Down the right-hand side there was a column in which people had recorded their impressions of the mountains. I opened the book near the middle. 'The bog is everywhere,' I read. 'There is no escaping it. But we praise God that nothing can separate us from the love of God which is in Christ.'

'Edward,' I said. 'Come and look at this.'

He staggered over, grabbed the book and began reading out loud. But his voice tailed off as he read on. When he had finished he muttered, 'Jesus' very quietly. He flicked over the pages, found another entry and handed the book back to me. 'Moose from Britain,' it said simply. 'Never again.'

There was a gap of several years in the entries. The Mountain Club had closed down altogether in the 1970s when Amin and then Obote were in power and had only started up again two years earlier. The latest entry of all had evidently been written by the man we had met in the Saad Hotel. 'Unbelievable,' it said. And then, in smaller letters underneath, in case this sounded too half-hearted, 'Fantastic.'

Edward had decided that he would take the crampons and an ice axe. Everything was ready. The porters loaded the equipment back into the pick-up and climbed in on top. Edward and I rode up in the front with Daniel. Moses was to drive us up to where the road ran out.

We hadn't gone more than a few hundred yards when the engine began to overheat. First wisps and then jets of steam hissed out from either side of the bonnet. Moses, who had watched the porters climb into the back while emitting little piping sounds of displeasure, did not hesitate. He insisted that they get out and walk. The porters did not care for this at all. Their attitude towards Moses was fast solidifying from confusion into hostility. They got off reluctantly and when the pick-up drove on, at walking pace, they held on to bits of the bodywork as if to slow it down.

There were corrugated iron mission churches dotted around the hillsides. On one side of the road a wooden trough carried water down to the village. After an hour the road led into a clearing surrounded by elephant grass. Moses braked hard to take the porters unawares and turned off the engine. 'The end of the road,' he said.

'I think I've got cerebral malaria,' said Edward.

'Do you? What makes you think that?'

'Very bad headache. And I feel feverish.'

Now I came to think of it I had a headache. Something was pounding away behind my temples, while my stomach felt as if it was being pulled rapidly back and forth through a trouser press. 'I don't feel very well either. Perhaps I've got it too.'

'Not a very good start is it?' said Edward.

The pangas were being handed out to the porters who waved them about and took a few swipes at the elephant grass which crumpled at a single blow. The mountains were covered in cloud, a greyish blue over the lower peaks darkening steadily the higher you got.

Daniel told the porters to get loaded up. They swung the sacks over their shoulders and adjusted the harnesses round their fore-heads. A number of them wore hats. One very tall man had what appeared to be a tea-cosy on his head – a little crocheted helmet in lilac coloured wool. All except Daniel were walking in bare feet. Their feet, though, didn't resemble any I was used to. They were enormous, largely due to a thick ridge of light skin that ran round the outside of each foot like the skirt on a hovercraft. The soles of their feet too were covered in slabs of dead skin. Their toes looked like afterthoughts. Not on account of their size – they were all up around the cotton-reel mark when it came to circumference – but the way in which they were stuck on the end of each great wedge of flesh.

Moses came to say goodbye. He shook our hands. 'I wish you much luck,' he said. His eyes darted off to the left where the porters were standing, waiting to move off. 'Be careful,' he added. 'Some of these men are not saved.' He started up the pick-up and pulled away back down the road.

The path led through the elephant grass down to a river. A tree had been felled and dragged across to form a bridge. The porters ran over, sacks bouncing on their backs. On the other side there was a house with a tin roof and a verandah, and beside it a larger building with a chimney. Smoke was pouring out of the chimney. All around there were rectangular shapes the size of cars, covered with tarpaulins. Some were already half overgrown with grass, others had been put there more recently.

A door opened in the building with a chimney. More smoke billowed out. As it cleared a man could be seen standing there, squinting at us in apparent disbelief. He waved away the last few trails of smoke and walked over. At first I thought his skin was very black, blacker than any I had seen, with a strange crystalline sparkle to it. It turned out that he was covered in soot. When he wiped his face streaks of light brown appeared underneath.

'Good morning to you,' he said. 'Good morning.' A look of panic came over him, as if he had exhausted his stock of pleasantries and was now in open conversational country. 'My name is Mr Sampson,' he said. He turned and walked towards the main building, stopping after a few yards and calling to us, 'Cold drink?'

The porters went on ahead. We followed Mr Sampson into a room where the chairs had been draped with polythene. A groundsheet too was spread on the floor. 'Soot,' he said. 'It gets everywhere.' He folded up two pieces of polythene and asked us to sit down.

'What are you doing here?' I asked.

'I am building a hotel,' he said. 'But first I have to make the bricks. I am doing it all myself. So far I have made 100,000 bricks. When I have made 250,000 then I will start to dig the foundations.' He poured out three glasses of lemonade and sat down in a chair whose shape had all but disappeared under several layers of polythene. They seemed to envelop him, the top few sheets closing over his chest.

'Can you be confident that people will come and stay in your hotel once it's built?'

'I am an optimist,' he said, wrapped in his polythene cocoon. 'I have been here for eight months now. I know I am taking a gamble. People have told me that I am mad. But they will be laughing ...' He stopped. He had forgotten the phrase he wanted. He clicked his fingers in frustration. A puff of soot rose from his hand. 'On the other sides of their faces when I am finished.'

On the wall there was a series of architects' plans of how the hotel would look. It was very grand. Two rows of pillars stretched either side of the front door, dormer windows were set into the roof. 'Fifteen rooms,' he said. 'Each with its own bathroom, of course. Ideally situated for walking tours. Tell me, where have you been staying?'

We said we'd been staying in the Margherita.

'Ah, terrible, isn't it? Did the lights go off?' We admitted they had. 'At mealtimes?' We nodded. He was smiling broadly now, his teeth as dark as his face. This was what he wanted to hear. 'And the food?' We said nothing. He sat back, his point made. 'Exactly. Bread and butter is not a proper starter.' This may have been true, but still I felt guilty of a betrayal. In the two days we had stayed there I had developed a sizeable soft spot for the Margherita. It was difficult to say why, except that I liked it precisely because the food was dreadful and the power went off and the carpet had been torn up, and yet everyone tried so hard. For me it was all impossibly exotic. For Ugandans, though, it was further evidence of what an appalling mess the country had fallen into.

'Don't you get lonely up here by yourself?' asked Edward.

'This is the news from London,' said Mr Sampson. He had a very good BBC voice – plummy, well-modulated, just the right note of lofty detachment. He pointed at a radio set in the corner. 'I listen to the World Service. It keeps me going. You know, when I was small I thought Bush House was like this, a little place in a clearing somewhere in the bush with all these people crowded round a microphone. Then one day I saw a photograph of it. I was shocked. It seemed quite wrong.'

We finished our lemonade and went outside. Mr Sampson said that he would like to cut us both sticks. But his panga was blunt. He chopped at some bamboos and then tried to pull them out of the ground, twisting and heaving without much success. Eventually we ended up with two thin, very mangled sticks that bent sharply whenever any pressure was put on them. Mr Sampson walked away down to the brick furnace. When he opened the door the smoke seemed to draw him back inside.

Daniel and the porters were waiting beyond the clearing. They had sat down in a circle, but sprang to their feet when they saw us coming. Daniel took one look at our sticks and told us to throw them away. He went off to cut us some more, returning with two thick, unbendable bamboo staves. I held mine up beside me like a pikestaff – it was several inches taller than I was. I felt stricken with nerves. I thought of Horace C. Holly – I was veering closer to Holly all the time. Although never in danger of losing his composure, Holly had sunk into gloom at the beginning of his trip, lying awake under the stars speculating on the pointlessness of thought and the futility of attempting to make sense of anything – when Holly agonised he liked to set himself a big agenda. 'What is the purpose of our feeble crying in the silence of space? Can our dim intelligence read the secrets of the star-strewn sky? Does any answer come out of it? Never any at all – nothing but echoes and fantastic visions!' He too had ventured up into the mountains burdened by major rhetorical questions.

The path led through a field of matoke into a clump of bamboos. A tangle of greenery closed in on either side, meeting above our heads. A number of men came down the path towards us. Most wore suits. A few carried umbrellas. They had come, said Daniel, from a funeral at one of the villages high up on the slopes. The man who had died was the elder of the village. He had been very old.

'How old?' we asked.

Daniel took some time to work this out. 'A hundred and twenty seven,' he said.

'That is extremely old,' said Edward.

All of his family – or at least most of them – had gathered for the funeral. This consisted of a large portion of the local population. The man had had well over thirty wives. He had outlived most of the early ones, but his latest brides were still in their teens. Apparently, towards the end there had been some confusion in his mind between his wives and his great-granddaughters. This could have been awkward. However, the local minister had stepped in to avert a crisis.

The funeral was in its third day. The obsequies were expected to go on for another two. Those people we passed on the path had ducked out early. The dead man had been very religious, a devout Christian who had contributed a great deal of money to the building of local churches. He had been saved. So too – despite Moses' suspicions – had almost all the porters. Daniel was chairman of his local church, a post that entailed his having to deliver two sermons a month. He also had a number of wives.

'How many?' we wanted to know.

He counted them off on his fingers. There were four. A fifth finger unclenched itself but was not properly extended.

'Four and a half?'

'Four.' He smiled – his lip got snagged again – 'but I have a mind to take a fifth. There is a girl I like very much. She is the sister of one of my other wives.'

'And do the other wives mind? Do they get jealous?'

'They are all happy,' he said. 'And they all love me. It is good for everyone.'

Being a Christian was no bar to taking a number of wives – at least not round here, where the missionaries who had arrived at the beginning of the century were so delighted at the conversion rate that they didn't want to spoil things by imposing too many moral restraints. Any marriages after the first tended not to be solemnised in church, but this didn't cause any bother. No one, of course, came out with it and said that the church condoned polygamy. They just kept quiet and hoped that a little expediency wouldn't get in the way of salvation.

In England, we explained, men were only allowed to take one wife at a time. The church, in particular, took a dim view of anyone who exceeded his quota. Daniel found this difficult to understand.

'Do many people go to church?' he asked.

'No,' we said. 'Not many.'

'Here everybody goes. When I speak in church people come from many miles.'

'What was the subject of your last sermon?'

'It was constancy,' said Daniel.

The porters had gone on ahead. They half ran rather than walked, the banana leaves taut round their foreheads, their faces quite expressionless. It had started to rain. Drops spattered on to the bamboos overhead and fell down the back of my neck. The path was rising, climbing the bank of a river that rushed and foamed below, throwing spray high up the trunks of trees alongside.

Daniel pointed out the village where the funeral was taking place. It was on the other side of the river towards the top of a ridge. Through the trees you could see a jumble of colours – clothing presumably – massed together between some huts. Everything though was quite still. There was no sign of any movement at all. Perhaps they were all bent in prayer. But after three days it was unlikely. A good deal of drink tended to be consumed at funerals. They might all have passed out.

Theirs was the highest village in the Ruwenzori. Only hunters and climbing parties went any further up into the mountains. But here, as in most of western Uganda, there was nothing much left to hunt. The area had once been plentiful in elephant, gorilla, buffalo and leopard. There were also blue monkey, bushbuck and what the botanist Patrick Synge called, 'stupendous chameleons' possessed of three horns.

'All gone,' said Daniel. He said it quite cheerfully, as if the last traces of a pestilence had finally been eradicated.

'Everything?'

Everything apart from occasional elephants who had wandered off course and were usually too old or sick to correct their mistake – and hyrax. These were the size of guinea pigs and, due to a particularly strange genetic condition, closely related to elephants. But even hyrax were pretty rare. Those people who still bothered to go hunting seldom came back with anything to brag about.

All around the bamboo grew taller and thicker. There was scarcely any light, still less sound, apart from the rustle of wind in the leaves high above. Rising up to 50 feet, the bamboo all but blotted out the sun and acted like a huge acoustic blanket. If you clapped your hands the sound waves seemed to shrivel in front of you. This was our first taste of gigantism. The bamboo here grew at the rate of 3 feet a day. In places it topped 100 feet.

130

No one had ever come up with a satisfactory explanation for why plants and vegetation grew to such dimensions in the Ruwenzori. Synge had speculated that it must have something to do with a fairly low and constant temperature, a very high humidity, a strong ultra-violet light intensity and a massive annual rainfall. But he admitted that he didn't really know and confessed himself baffled by just how many of the plants ever got on to the mountains in the first place.

The damp had brought the insects out. They swarmed round our heads, a ball of tiny black flecks that hummed and hovered in perfect formation, regrouping instantly they'd been swatted away. There were larger insects too that circled round the others, keeping watch. The air was heavy and smelled of things rotting away underfoot. In places the path was so narrow that you had to squeeze sideways between the bamboos. It was like walking down a deep ravine, a seamless world of light green broken only by fat purple slugs that clung to the stems of the bamboo and the thin muddy path that snaked out ahead.

When the Mountain Club was in its heyday, back in the 1950s and early 1960s, paths were kept open all year round. Parties with pangas would be despatched to hack back the undergrowth. Huts too had been built for climbers to stay in and fitted out with beds and stoves. Most of the paths were now completely overgrown. Some were barely passable in places. No one seemed too sure about the state of the huts.

Up ahead I could see Edward, stooped in his anorak, climbing up the side of a gulley. He was having to clutch on to tree roots and haul himself up on the strings of liannas that dangled over the edge.

When I got to the top and looked over the other side there was no sign of him. There was no path either. A mud-slide had carried half the hillside away. Somewhere towards the bottom – 20 feet or so down the slope – several lumps of mud like boulders were piled around the base of a banana tree. Along with the bamboo, the banana tree had gone in for some vigorous mutating. Its leaves were the size of ceremonial flags, hanging down to the ground. Any bananas – there weren't any – would have been as big as canoes.

'Edward,' I called out. 'Where are you?'

It was like shouting into a mattress.

One of the huge leaves twitched and drew aside.

'How did you get up there?'

'I fell,' said Edward. 'I fell down the hill.' He was brushing mud from his trousers.

'Are you all right?'

'Of course I'm all right. I'm fine.'

Daniel was picking his way down the mud-slide. There was a depressing nimbleness about the way he did everything.

'What happened?' he asked.

'I fell,' said Edward.

'Edward fell over,' I repeated. I didn't want this moment to go away. We had suffered an accident. Admittedly no one had been hurt and besides, it hadn't even happened to me. That, though, was the trouble. I wished it had. I saw myself cartwheeling down the slope, feet over my head, overcome with relief at having something tangible to complain about.

'You could have broken something. Our whole trip might have had to be aborted.'

'Nonsense. I'm not even bruised.'

He wasn't making a fuss. I realised how much I detested stoicism. Presented with a prime opportunity to vent some anguish, Edward had passed it up. I would not have been so careless.

Daniel had moved off, skipping down the remains of the hillside to where the greenery took hold once more.

'Tell me, Edward,' I was struggling to cram my voice back into its normal register. 'Isn't this much tougher than you expected?'

'I suppose it is, a bit.'

'A bit? Be honest with me for God's sake. I mean look at this place.'

The bamboos soared overhead, bending towards one another to form a vault above us. Stray raindrops, fatted with malice, dropped from the uppermost fronds and thudded on to my back.

'It won't go on for ever,' said Edward.

'It won't?' I wanted assurances. 'How do you know?'

'This is the bamboo forest. It only goes up to 7,000 feet.'

132

'And then what happens?'

'Then we get into the podocarpus forest.'

'What's that?'

'I'm not quite sure.'

We followed Daniel, scrambling across the mud. The same thing had happened in the next three gulleys, great slabs of land had sheared off and now clung to the hillside, the bamboos sprouting horizontally or even upside-down. After an hour of this I asked Daniel if we might stop for some food. He looked unhappy. We were already falling behind, he said. We must try to go faster. He swung his arms and stamped his feet to show what he meant. The food anyway was all with the porters. There was nothing to eat. We sat down by the edge of a stream and drank some water.

When Synge had come here in 1936 he had noted what a depressing place it was – despite being much taken by the dimensions of the bamboo. The atmosphere had rubbed off on to the porters who grew steadily more sullen and then staged a strike, demanding more money. Synge and his party decided that they must not give in to blackmail and mounted a show of strength. Two or three of the porters were 'mercilessly stripped' of their clothing and told to go home. This had the desired effect. The rest of them abandoned their demands. Morale, however, did not improve much. Synge wished he'd brought a wind-up gramophone to cheer everyone up.

'Your blood-sugar level is very low,' said Edward. 'Your face has gone very white.' He peered at me more closely. 'Practically blue.' He turned to Daniel. 'Don't you think John is a strange colour?' But Daniel had already jumped the stream and was waiting for us to catch up.

The bamboo began to thin out. Narrow slits of light showed through the trunks and broadened as we walked up another long green gulch. We came out into the open at the junction of three great ridges. The ground dropped away to the left and right. Far below, the river we had skirted earlier was a narrow band of mercury strung through the trees. The hills were covered with bracken and vast knots of vegetation that reared up into the air like stormheads. The sky was an uncertain sort of blue, thin and watery and scudded with shreds of cloud. Above us was another ridge, far steeper than anything we had climbed so far. You had to lean back to see the top of it. Ranged right along the top was a single row of trees with the sky showing through behind. They looked like Indian braves gazing down on a wagon train, just biding their time. 'We are going up there,' said Daniel, pointing at the trees. The porters had already made it. A line of tiny bobbing shapes was jogging along the skyline.

Daniel decided that Edward should go first. He would follow while I brought up the rear. They were already pulling ahead by the time we'd gone a few yards. I couldn't keep up. Every few paces I had to rest, leaning on my stick and gasping for air. Edward and Daniel were walking together. I could hear snatches of their conversation being blown down the hill without quite making out what was being said. But I knew. I knew exactly what they were talking about. It had to be me. My glaring deficiencies in all areas of physical endeavour – it was an irresistible topic.

Periodically Edward and Daniel would wait for me to catch up. By the time I made it they were looking perfectly composed, under no apparent strain. Daniel, though, had his lip hooked round the gap in his teeth. No longer in amusement but concern.

'Daniel was asking if you were baptised,' said Edward.

'What for?'

'He was wondering about our religious beliefs. He wants to know if you're a good Christian.'

I didn't have the breath to ask any more questions. Besides, all this religious mania was getting me down. But as we set off again it struck me why Daniel had been so curious. He thought I might die. That had to be it. He thought I might die and he wanted to be able to bury me with due decorum – at least he wanted to find out if I warranted it. The thought angered me so much that for a while it spurred me to greater effort. But not for long. Soon the ground had opened up between us once more as I stumbled about through the ferns, beset by paranoia and resentment.

It developed into quite a pattern. They would set off, I would lag behind, they would wait for me. On one such occasion Edward said, 'I thought you were fit. You told me you were going to a gym.'

By then I was unable to say anything. I was slipping down my stick too, bent almost double as I gasped for air. And anyway, I had been to a gym.

It was in a basement off Tottenham Court Road. Beaming with bogus affability the girl behind the reception desk had asked me to get changed. Someone would be along shortly to devise a suitable exercise programme for me. She said it as if she were addressing a small child, all but swamped beneath a welter of learning difficulties.

There were two full-length mirrors in the changing room. In front of each one was a naked man. They were talking about the standard of service in some restaurant. 'Forty-five minutes for a piece of veal,' said one, inclining his leg forward to admire the musculature. The other one grizzled in sympathy and beat himself on the chest with the flat of his hand. Rather harder than he had intended by the look of it. A large red mark began to show through his chest hair.

I had brought a special vest for the occasion with cutaway sleeves to accommodate what would soon be a pair of amply swelling biceps. But when I put it on I was appalled to see that it exposed one or other of my nipples, depending on which arm I moved. Another man came in exuding the same cheery insincerity as the receptionist – he was shimmering with it. He explained that I would have to do various tests to gauge my level of fitness. I pedalled about for a while on a bicycle with no wheels, did as many press-ups as I could manage, and blew down what looked like the tube of a vacuum cleaner until everything in my line of sight began to develop a shimmering orange penumbra.

There was one more test. For this we had to go into the gymnasium. A treadmill was standing against a wall, a 4-foot rubber belt with guide-rails on either side. The speed of the belt could be controlled by a button set into one of the rails. A digital counter showed how many meters you'd covered.

'I want you to run 800 metres,' said the man. He started the machine. The belt began to move backwards under my feet. When it had reached what he considered a suitable speed he wandered off, saying that he'd be back in a couple of minutes.

Unaccustomed to the rhythm, my body flailed about desperately as I tried to bring my arms somewhere into line with the movement of my legs. It was much more difficult than I had anticipated. Over in the other corner of the gym a girl was pulling angrily at the handles of a rowing machine. I looked down at the distance counter. It was hard to believe I had only covered 120 metres.

The thing was going way too fast for me. My hand groped along the guide-rail trying to find the control. There only seemed to be one button. I pressed it. The rubber belt began to move faster. I pressed it again. There was a further acceleration. My legs were now whirling around so fast that I could no longer be sure just who was in charge. They had developed a desperate momentum of their own, threatening to separate from my torso at any moment.

I pressed the button once again, frantically jabbing at it with my forefinger. The belt went into overdrive. There was a clunking noise as it engaged an entirely new set of gears. My legs suddenly gave way. I felt myself being borne backwards at tremendous speed. It was my last wholly conscious impression. But I remember a great sheet of flame that seemed to leap up behind my eyes just as my head hit the wall.

I could see Edward and Daniel standing over me. Beside them the man in the crocheted lilac hat was trying to get the stopper out of a bottle. He was pulling it with his teeth. There was something hard under my back. I was lying on a rock, tilted up so that I looked down across the sea of bracken to where the three smaller ridges met below.

Daniel said, 'Abraham has got something for you.'

The man in the hat had got the stopper out. He put the bottle to my lips and tipped it up. Something thick and sweet slid down my throat.

'It's honey,' said Edward. 'It'll make you feel better.'

'What happened?'

'Have you got blurred vision?' Edward had a book with a red plastic cover open in his hand.

'No.'

'Are you shivering?'

'Yes.'

'Are you incapable of sustaining a single line of thought or topic of conversation?'

'I don't know.'

'Well, try.'

'What do you want me to talk about?'

'What are the Thirty-Nine Steps?'

'The Thirty-Nine Steps is an organisation dedicated to the overthrow – I can't remember what they were trying to overthrow.'

'I think you're suffering from exhaustion,' said Edward, closing the book. 'You collapsed. You looked like you'd been shot in the legs.'

A number of the other porters were also staring down at me. I saw that they no longer had the banana leaves round their foreheads. One of them was sipping from a mug.

'Where are we?'

'We are in the podocarpus forest. The camp isn't far away.'

Edward and Abraham helped me to my feet. They let go of me gingerly, their hands hovering inches from my shoulders in case I fell again. When we moved off the porters dropped into two lines behind, walking slowly and suspiciously, like elderly pall-bearers.

The ground fell away almost sheer on either side. An avenue of trees ran down the centre of the ridge towards a clearing where a fire was smouldering. On the other side of the fire was the remains of a corrugated iron hut. The door had been pulled off its hinges and one of the walls was buckled as if something had charged into it.

I collapsed on the ground, dry-retching in that apologetic sort of way that cats do when they've got fur stuck in their throats. Edward brought me a cup of milky orange liquid with lumps of undissolved powder floating around on the surface. I didn't need to ask what this was. I licked the remainder of the honey from my lips before taking my first mouthful of Joe Weider's Dynamic Carbo-Energiser. It didn't taste of anything much, cheap fruit crush that's been over-diluted. Still, I drained the cup and lay back waiting for a great jolt of revitalisation.

Nothing happened. I drank two more cups, hoping that at any moment I would leap to my feet, tingling with keenness. There was no effect at all. At least nothing I could discern, until I went for a pee and discovered that my penis had turned a dark shade of navy blue.

This took quite a while to sink in. But there could be no doubt about it. An unnaturally pigmented thing was hanging from my flies. I rolled it around between my fingers trying to restore some circulation – to no avail.

'You're very quiet,' said Edward, after I'd sat down again.

'I've got a lot on my mind.'

I wondered what to do. It was a difficult subject to broach, even with a friend. On the other hand, it seemed the sort of condition that was unlikely to get better of its own accord. For the time being I did nothing. Later I discovered that my thighs too were blue, as if the blood had drained away, sunk down towards my feet. The damp had made the dye in my trousers run. My skin was navy blue from my waist down to my ankles.

The light was beginning to fade. To the north there were snow-capped peaks just visible on the horizon. The porters were stretched out round the fire, some already wrapped in their cotton blankets. A large metal pot full of water was balanced on the edge of the fire. When the water boiled, one of the men poured in quantities of cassava flour. Almost immediately it turned into a thick grey porridge. Two men with a long wooden spoon were needed to stir it. They stood up to get a better grip on the spoon, looking like they were trying to steer a boat in particularly difficult conditions.

Daniel brought out several bundles of dried fish wrapped in paper and handed them round. The fish were quite stiff, their tails bent over in a circle. When the blending was finished the porters broke off pieces of fish and dipped them in the porridge. And when the fish was all gone they ate the porridge by itself, running their fingers round the side of the pot.

We pitched the tent. Edward had decided that we would cook tortellini. He ladled them out of the saucepan on to two plates and handed me one.

'You must try and eat something.'

But the idea of food revolted me. Especially tortellini. Whenever I looked at the plate I could only think of one thing. The tortellini looked exactly like babies' ears. Neatly severed, even cutely crinkled, but babies' ears just the same. I managed to eat one. It was spongy and moist and went down into my stomach under strong protest. In the end I forced myself to nibble round the edges of a few of the tortellini, never getting too near the little parcels of meat. That way it felt as if I was only eating the tops of the babies' ears and not the lobes.

There was no sunset, scarcely any twilight. By half past seven it was dark. We got into our sleeping bags. Edward was reading Osmaston and Pasteur's *Guide to the Ruwenzori* by the light of his torch. Published in 1972, this tells you everything you need to know to go walking in the Mountains of the Moon, including the Swahili for 'Yes, there are no bananas.'

'I think tomorrow might be easier,' said Edward. He read out a brief résumé of what we could expect. 'The path . . . drops steeply to the river which is crossed by the Busk suspension bridge.' This had been put up in 1958, the same year as the first Uganda ski championships had been held – the Ski Club of Uganda prided itself on being one of the most exclusive and undersubscribed clubs in the world. I liked the thought of a suspension bridge. Somehow it was a very comforting image. I clung to it as I went to sleep.

I dreamed of fleeing down a slope to a river at the bottom, tumbling through the undergrowth, my heart pounding in panic. There were brambles scratching my face and hands. Behind me I could hear the babies closing in fast, a chubby pink army crying for vengeance. They wanted their ears back, of course. I made it on to the suspension bridge. It was an exceptionally beautiful bridge of the palest hemp, woven across the river.

The babies were right on my heels now. On the other side of the bridge I could see Daniel. He had his head thrown back, exposing the gap in his teeth, and was holding up something metallic that caught the sun. As I got closer he swung himself forward, bringing his panga down on the guy-ropes anchoring the bridge to the riverbank.

Ten

I could see the sky lightening through the walls of the tent. The porters were already up. There were sounds of hushed talking and pots being rinsed in the water butt. I'd lain awake for most of the night, my stomach mashing about in an acidic frenzy, fingers inching out towards the valium bottle. But I was determined to save these until later; they were something to look forward to. Edward rolled over and stared at his watch. His arm flopped back on to his sleeping bag.

'How do you feel?' he asked.

It was a case of picking on a word that denoted enfeeblement without implying lack of spirit. 'Weak,' I said.

Edward grunted. He said, 'The thing to do is pretend that this is your last day on Earth.'

I stopped, halfway out of my sleeping bag.

'What do you mean?'

The possibility that this might all end in bloodshed hadn't previously struck me. Still, there could be little doubt that I was shaping up to be an extremely trying companion. A showdown of some kind couldn't be ruled out.

'Well,' said Edward, 'if it was your last day on Earth then you'd try and enjoy it, wouldn't you?'

I agreed that I would, though more out of surprise than conviction. And the more I thought about it, the more flawed an argument this seemed. Twenty-four hours left to extinction wasn't my idea of a time for merriment. On the contrary, it sounded like a powerful excuse for some really impassioned moaning; a final crescendo of complaint.

Edward was trying to find the World Service on his radio. The aerial swung around the tent like an *épée*. There was a lot of crackling and then a very faint voice that said, 'The udders become distended and sore.' Immediately afterwards the static closed in again.

Outside, Daniel was standing looking up at the sky. He was keen to get going. Dark banks of cloud were converging overhead. 'Rain?' I asked.

He nodded. There was a prolonged booming from down the valley to our right.

'Thunder?'

He nodded again.

'Thunderstorm?'

He shrugged. 'Maybe.' At least he wasn't sure. This was a relief of sorts.

'Maybe thunderstorm, maybe tempest,' he said.

The porters' gear was all packed up, the sacks leaning against one another in a circle. But there was no sign of the porters themselves. As we sat drinking tea they came out of the woods into the clearing, converging as if from equally spaced points on a compass, looking neither to left nor right but heading straight for the pile of sacks.

'Where have the porters been?'

Daniel pulled at his beard. 'They have been to the lavatory.'

Edward had measured five times the recommended dose of Carbo-Energiser into a thermos flask. He screwed on the lid and handed it to me to put in my rucksack.

'Tell me,' I said. 'Just how would you define a tempest?'

'It's a storm of apocalyptic proportions. Why do you ask?'

'It doesn't matter.'

We would go on first, said Daniel. The porters could catch up later. The way he said this suggested they wouldn't find it any great problem. They weren't going to be left eating dust.

'Remember,' said Edward, as we walked out of the clearing and down to the edge of the ridge, 'your last day on Earth.'

One thing soon became clear. It was going to be a long day. I had no idea that walking downhill could be so difficult. I tried it forwards, then sideways and finally backwards in a series of robust squat-jumps that had Daniel calling out in alarm. The Carbo-Energiser sloshed about on my back. There was a tangle of stalks and creepers that

142

fastened round my feet at every step. It was like walking into an endless succession of man-traps.

Halfway down the ridge the porters came past. They looked completely unconcerned about anything, disappearing downhill at such speed that all trace of them was gone in a few seconds. The nearer we got to the bottom the louder the sound of the river became and the more I looked forward to seeing the suspension bridge.

But the bridge had gone. There wasn't even anything to show where it had once been. The river had turned into a torrent. White water foamed between two tall cliffs and cascaded on to slabs of black rock. I took the absence of the bridge very badly. I felt cheated. I started protesting to Daniel and pointing out the page in Osmaston and Pasteur where the bridge had been mentioned.

'Washed away,' he said.

'How long ago?'

He didn't know. 'A long time.'

The porters were standing around waiting for us. We would have to cross on foot. I sat down on the bank, pulling at my boot laces. Abraham and another of the porters stepped into the river. They jumped effortlessly from stone to stone. Edward was next. He too had little difficulty, jabbing his stick in the water to balance himself. He sprang off the last rock on to the opposite bank.

'You will go next,' said Daniel.

I hung my boots round my neck. Across the river I could see Abraham and Edward sitting on the bank, their sticks propped beside them. There was something about the way they looked I didn't like. As I stepped into the water I realised what it was. They looked expectant, geared up for entertainment.

The water swelled round my ankles. My feet slithered about on the wet rock until I got a grip. I made the first three stepping stones and launched myself at the fourth. It was shaped like a bowl with a dip in the middle. To my surprise I made it. But my balance wasn't good. I was wavering, hinged loosely at the hip, my spine arching back one moment and hunched forward the next.

I looked around for the next rock to aim at. There wasn't one – not a rock in sight I could possibly reach. I was stuck. I could see

Edward and Abraham, through a cloud of spray. They were shouting at me, but their words were lost in the roar of the current. The water was paralysingly cold. The feeling in my legs was beginning to ebb away. I checked to see that there really wasn't a rock within reach. Not a thing. Well, that was it then. I'd just have to stay here. And strangely enough, it didn't seem so bad; more a relief than anything else. I looked at the ridges covered with trees and the river that rushed past down through the valley. There was a lot to be said for holding out against the common purpose, for being deaf to all entreaties. It had its compensations. All I wanted was to be left alone. They could go on without me. I didn't care. I was making my stand.

There were signs of activity on the bank. Edward had got up, but Abraham had already beaten him to it. I saw with a stab of annoyance that he was coming for me. By now he must have been getting pretty used to seeing me *in extremis*. He stepped back into the current and was holding the end of his stick out towards me. I could see it wriggling around as he got closer. Now everyone was shouting from both banks. They must have stepped up the volume because I could hear cries of encouragement coming from behind.

Abraham too was calling out. He had his stick fully extended. I had no interest in grabbing for it at all. I was happy enough. I remembered how, as a child, few pleasures had matched that of dropping the baton in a relay race; the side let down, camaraderie sabotaged. Abraham's smile had disappeared. His face had clouded over with concern. He couldn't understand why I wasn't helping him out.

He was very close by now, the black end of his stick was only a couple of feet away. The cries of encouragement were turning to cries of anger. A harsher tone altogether was cutting through the water rush. Somehow it seemed churlish, at least not to make an effort. I lunged forward and caught hold of the stick. Abraham pulled sharply. I felt as if I was running across the surface of the water and then there were stones under my feet once more.

No one said anything. I couldn't blame them. There wasn't really that much to say. I sat down and put my boots back on. The other porters crossed over, one after the other in rapid succession. None of them said anything either. When they got to the bank they looked at me and dropped their heads in embarrassment. Daniel was last. He wanted to know what had happened. He looked round for an explanation.

The porters stood, stooped under their loads and stared at their feet. I gazed at a point over Daniel's left shoulder where I suspected the bridge had once been. After a while he told the porters to get moving. All except Abraham. Daniel called him over. They half turned away. Daniel was talking to him, his lips close to his ear. Abraham nodded gravely.

As we started up the slope it became clear that Abraham had been assigned to shadow me, to ensure that I didn't get into any more trouble. He walked alongside, reining himself back to keep pace with me. His feet hung in the air between each step. He kept shooting sidelong glances at me to make sure I wasn't outfoxing him with any sudden variations in pace. The effort was taking it out of him. He wasn't used to going this slowly. I could see beads of sweat standing out on his forehead either side of his bandanna of banana leaves. He laughed too whenever I caught him looking at me. It was a high-pitched, rather girlish sort of laugh triggered by any kind of eye contact. He kept it up until I looked away again.

The path climbed through the trees. The ground was almost bare underfoot, a thick crust of mud veined with little rivulets. Overhead, the greenery grew thicker, blotting out the sun once more. Whatever obduracy I'd shown, momentarily, in the middle of the river had gone, to be succeeded first by shame and then by something more pervasive still – persecution mania. Everyone was against me. There could be no doubt about that. Everyone and everything, even the vegetation. There were small stubby branches that stuck out from the trees at head height. You'd duck under one and come up sharply under another. The entire landscape was bristling with aggression.

I tried to convince myself that it was quite permissible to think like this. People were constantly returning from desolate spots, raving about the malevolence of inanimate things. The difference was that they'd invariably been away for months in conditions of severe deprivation. I was like this after one and a half days. I couldn't even reassure myself that I had altitude sickness yet. It didn't strike until at least 12,000 feet. We were still 1,000 feet short.

But my lack of fortitude appalled me the most. I had always hoped that in moments of crisis I might prove equal to any challenge demanded. Latent reserves of resolution, even courage would spring to the fore. The odds, though, were heavily stacked against it. I hadn't realised just how heavily stacked until several months earlier.

It was a weekday afternoon in Covent Garden. The streets were full of shoppers. Sprinting towards me, carving a path through the pedestrians came a thin dark man clutching a woman's handbag to his chest. There was an expression of billowing exultation on his face. His cheeks were inflated, his eyes bright. He was running flat out, but still paying some attention to where he put his feet. The pavement was slippery, he didn't want to fall over.

From down the street came a woman's voice. 'Stop that man. He's got my bag.' And then, more plaintively, 'Help me, someone.'

There was ample time. He was 10 yards away. It was just a case of sticking out a leg. Even a shove might have done it. And time was stretching out to accommodate me. Everything became infuriatingly slow. The man looked as if he was going to grind to a halt right by my side, still straining for motion but failing to get any grip. I was imploring him to get a move on. Then, as he drew level, everything quickened again. He picked up pace and sped away.

A heavily built woman in T-shirt and jeans panted hopelessly after him. She was falling behind with every step.

All down the street I was pleased to see people were following my example. They shrank into doorways pretending to be preoccupied with the window displays. It was as if a little cyclone had passed by. The effort of simulated confusion had really taken it out of us. We shuffled off, avoiding each others' eyes. I took the precaution of limping heavily until I turned a corner.

Afterwards, I thought how different it might all have been. The leg firmly extended, the thief falling through the air, the expressions of gratitude, the protestations on my part that it had all been nothing – I felt I could have hit just the right note of modesty. But it hadn't happened. That was the big drawback. And now, as I plodded up another savage gradient with Abraham by my side, I realised that I'd done it again. I'd miscalculated badly, entirely misjudged the size of the gap. There were no white-robed immortals here, no eighty-five copper statues from whose mouths the Nile spewed forth. How could there be? This wasn't the Africa I knew – a vast backdrop against which Europeans could act out their romances, covering themselves in self-proclaimed glory. This was a different place entirely.

No longer a landscape of the imagination, it had turned out to be like something from an outward-bound catalogue. A test of stamina and moral fibre. But I knew what sort of state my moral fibre was in. It was like a curtain of fine noodles. Anything coming the other way – anything at all – would sweep straight through it.

Abraham was laughing at me again, this time without any eye-contact to set him off. He sounded more nervous than usual too, as if his responsibilities were making him jittery. When I stopped to get my breath he said, 'Is everything all right?'

'All right? Why do you ask?'

'You were making a noise, sir.' This was the first time he had called me 'sir'. It felt like a barrier he had erected between us.

'What sort of noise?'

'It was a crying noise,' he said. 'Like an animal.'

'Are you sure?'

'Oh yes, sir,' he said sadly.

I wanted to get this straight. 'I was making a noise, you say? A crying noise?'

He nodded, his tea-cosy hat bobbing up and down. This was worse than I'd thought. Not that it hadn't happened before. It had. I'd just hoped the consequences might have prevented any recurrence.

My trips to the British Museum Reading Room with Edward had tailed off some years earlier. Eventually it had proved impossible to stop him from seeing the first chapters of my Polish novel. He read through the thin sheaf of papers and said, 'I find your lead character rather unsympathetic.' I was astonished. The man had no personality at all, so how could he be sympathetic or unsympathetic? He was a completely transparent being, a hopeless nonentity, stuck forever in a wet flatland of indeterminate root vegetables.

But still I kept going on my own, at increasingly rare intervals. It wasn't as if my attempts at writing were going any better. On the contrary, they were getting worse. I just didn't seem able to keep away.

The Reading Room was crowded. All around people were bent over their work, lost in their own separate worlds. I asked for both volumes of Sir Samuel Baker's *The Albert Nyanza* and found one of the few remaining places to sit. The Polish novel had long since been abandoned. Now I was planning a short story completely devoid of human content, or indeed any recognisable signs of life. That way, I figured, I could neatly sidestep problems with characterisation. There had been a lot of stories like this lately. Usually they just concentrated on what was on the radio. But still it didn't come easily. It scarcely came at all. My short story was shorter than I'd ever anticipated. It was practically a haiku.

'Ssshh.'

There was a woman sitting on my left. She had twisted round and was hissing. It took me a moment to realise this was directed at me. I caught her eye and moved my head from one side to the other to see if her gaze drifted elsewhere. It did not. She was clearly mad. Another lunatic. It was extraordinary the way they sought me out. I took no notice. She looked exasperated and went back to her work.

I stared at my blank sheet of paper. How come it was so difficult? If everyone else was at it, surely it couldn't be that hard? The quality of my inner life was a major disappointment. And it wasn't just quality. There was size too; negligible activity within shrinking boundaries. You could really get depressed thinking about it.

'Ssshh. Please.'

She was doing it again. Perhaps it wasn't that surprising. You got a lot of odd people in a place like this.

'I'm sorry,' I said. I whispered it, so as not to disturb anyone else.

'Ssshh,' she hissed again.

I gave her an extended glare. The message, I hoped, was clear. Don't try and unsettle me with your pathetic delusions. I went back to more important things. How did I manage to do it? To be so unproductive? Something must have gone wrong. There were disconnected tubes flailing around in my head. Perhaps I needed an operation. Something drastic. For God's sake lighten up, I kept telling myself. But it was no good. When I was in this kind of mood all paths led sharply downhill.

A hand was placed on my shoulder. I looked up to see a man in uniform standing above me. He had a cap on with a twist of braid above the peak.

'Would you mind coming with me, sir.'

I realised at once what had happened. A complaint must have been made about the disturbance and somehow I'd been mistaken for the culprit. Under the circumstances it seemed best to go and explain. The mad woman was looking at me with a triumphant expression on her face. I gave her chair a little kick as I went past.

The man took me to an office opposite the lavatories. He listened to my story – how I was being persecuted by a maniac – and then said, 'But she says she was trying to get you to be quiet, sir.'

The duplicity of these people. How did they live with themselves?

'But I wasn't doing anything,' I told him.

'She said you were groaning, sir.'

'Groaning? Of course I wasn't groaning.'

'I'm afraid she wasn't the only one to complain, sir.' He consulted a piece of paper. 'Repeated groaning.'

Something small and cold clutched at my heart.

'Groaning?'

'Yes, sir.'

'Are you quite sure?'

'Positive,' he said. And then he added, 'I heard it myself.'

Involuntary groaning. Had it really come to this? Internal organs voicing despair of their own accord? This was self-betrayal on a scale never before encountered.

The man offered me a pill. I assumed it must be a tranquilliser. Surely they couldn't forcibly sedate me? Perhaps they could. The British Museum was very much a law unto itself. He held out his hand.

'Antacid, sir. For your stomach.'

Still in a state of shock, I wandered upstairs to where the Egyptian mummies were kept. There they were, lying on their palettes, neatly trussed up, looking ready to be airfreighted off somewhere. I stopped in front of one of the glass cases. On the side was a notice giving details of the mummy and the method of its preservation. The mummy's brain had, so the notice stated with no suggestion of anything unusual, been removed through its nose. Through its nose? Nothing else summed up so well the fragility of one's persona. Blow too hard and you could sneeze the whole thing out.

Now it had happened again; internal clamourings, voices raised in protest. I knew I wasn't going to be able to make it. The realisation had been dawning on me for the last couple of hours. Every few steps I was having to rest. Abraham hovered beside me. I couldn't bear to look at him any more. It wasn't so much the pity or concern on his face that bothered me, as the confusion. This kind of behaviour was way outside anything he'd ever witnessed. He was at a loss how to deal with it.

I could see Edward, not far away, but climbing easily, crouched forward against the slope like a spider. Occasionally he would turn round and wave. I didn't have the energy to wave back. It was going to be difficult to tell him. He wouldn't take it at all well. Still, my mind was made up. It seemed best to get it over with as soon as possible.

We stopped for lunch on a large flat rock. The porters sat round the edge while I sprawled out in the middle. Daniel, I noticed, didn't sit down. Looking preoccupied, he had walked off into the undergrowth. We had brought cheddar cheese and toasted muesli to eat. But the bags had burst and the muesli had stuck to the lumps of cheese. They tasted like rancid flapjacks. I managed to force one down, my gorge rising to meet it.

'Look, Edward. I don't really think I'm up to this.'

'What do you mean?'

'Well, I'm not sure if I can go on.'

There was a long pause after which Edward said very quietly, in a voice devoid of all confidence, 'Of course you can.'

'I can't. You know it too. Look at me.'

There was another, even longer pause. And then Edward said, 'What do you want to do?'

'I don't know . . . I'm sorry.' This was terrible. I was on the verge of tears. Everyone was blurring round the edges. The porters had sensed there was a crisis going on. They sat very still, not saying anything. Edward twisted his fingers round the straps of his rucksack. He kept shaking his head, as if to dislodge what I'd said from his mind. Daniel walked back to the rock and sat down.

'I've got malaria,' he said.

A ripple of concern ran round the rock. 'Malaria?' echoed Edward. He couldn't believe it.

Daniel was shivering slightly under his jacket, pulling the folds together across his chest. 'Pills,' he said looking at me. 'Do you have pills?'

At least he wouldn't find me wanting here. I shook the sacks, listening for the rattle of medicaments. They practically took up a sack on their own. The pill bottles were set out on the rock. I tipped out two malaria tablets and gave them to Daniel with the thermos of Carbo-Energiser. He snapped his head back and washed them down. Another shudder ran through him. He took deep breaths for a minute or so and then announced, 'I will be all right.'

The porters meanwhile were looking at the pill bottles and murmuring excitedly amongst themselves. There was a particularly large bottle of Panadol standing on the middle of the rock. One of them picked it up. 'What are these for?' he asked.

'They are for headaches.'

He pointed at his forehead. 'I have a headache.'

I shook out a couple of pills and gave them to him. He refused any liquid, chewing them instead so that he had a chalky white deposit round his lips. Behind him the other porters had formed into what appeared to be a queue. The next man complained that he too had a headache. He held out his hands, cupped together. The man behind him stood peering at the bottles before making up his mind.

'Headache and malaria,' he said. Fired by his example all the other men claimed similar afflictions. Even Abraham did not stint himself, eagerly asking for a double ration.

'My God,' I whispered to Edward as I handed out the pills. 'This is brilliant. These guys are even bigger hypochondriacs than we are.'

'It certainly looks that way,' he said.

The porters were all dosed up now. When I put the pill bottles back in the sack their eyes swung after them.

'What do you want to do?' said Edward.

'About what?'

'About going on. What do you think?'

Somehow this show of fallibility had done wonders for my morale. I felt immensely cheered, both by Daniel's malaria and the porters' fondness for pills. A pharmaceutical bond was taking shape. Nothing much as yet, it was still a start. Something to build on.

'I've decided to carry on,' I said.

'Are you sure?'

'No,' I said. 'Of course I'm not sure.'

The rain started, whipping in flurries as the clouds bore down the valley. There wasn't much left of the path by now. You had to scramble over boulders and across massive tree roots that erupted from the hillside in thick black coils. The pangas were useless. A chain-saw wouldn't have been much better. Thunder clapped close by, the echoes bouncing from one side of the valley to the other. Behind me Daniel coughed, his head sunk between his upturned lapels. I kept thinking of Patrick Synge who had written of this 'monstrous and unearthly landscape . . . like some imaginary reconstruction of life in a long past geological age, or even upon another planet.'

So far there hadn't been much that was monstrous or unearthly, only arduous. But things were changing rapidly. The trees, which until now had been straight-trunked and tall, looked as if they'd been struck by a particularly violent form of palsy. This was the giant heather. Branches were gnarled and grotesquely twisted. In places they had wrapped themselves round their own trunks as if they were

152

trying to throttle the life out of them. Most had huge dripping goitres of moss growing from them with holes in the centre like sphincters.

When the rain eased up briefly, the mist came down. You couldn't see more than about 20 feet in any direction. The light was grey and flat. It made everything look two-dimensional; insecurely anchored to the ground, ready to blow over at any moment. Up ahead I thought I could see a group of men standing quite erect and some way apart from each other. They turned out to be giant lobelias – 6 to 8 feet tall brown obelisks a foot across, tapering sharply towards the top. There were giant groundsels too, up to 10 feet high with straight hairy trunks like the necks of llamas. They bulged out near the top, as if some blockage had got caught in their throats, and were crowned with a spray of stiff pointed leaves.

The porters, said Daniel, did not like it here. They were moving more quickly than ever, but no longer with the same easy scampering gait. Now they looked hurried, their rhythm gone. Abraham had rejoined the others. It wasn't clear whether Daniel thought I no longer needed watching or Abraham had decided that he couldn't stand it anymore.

As we went on the trees grew increasingly festooned with lichen. It hung down from the branches, in single streamers at first then thickening into wispy grey green veils that billowed out when a gust caught them. In places the trees were completely shrouded. They looked like figures rearing up under blankets. 'We are coming close to the place of beards,' said Daniel. Apparently we had already gone past Kanyasabu, the place of mud.

Now I was stopping every few paces to reassure myself that this was real. Synge, who I'd begun to suspect was an excitable type, easily impressed, hadn't been exaggerating at all. I'd been looking for a dreamscape and here it was. This, though, was every bit as sinister as it was strange. Few Victorian illustrators had envisioned a wicked wood quite as bad as this one. There a sullenness over everything, an overwhelming sense of nature pushed way over the edge, its only common purpose being to shrug off any human imprint. Everything looked wrong, inverted. The trees didn't even make sense. You couldn't work out how the things stayed upright. A great

153

mass of branches erupted from a single trunk, flailing across the path, twisted and swollen with huge carbuncles. Nothing stirred. There was no noise, no birdsong, nothing except the rain on the leaves and the squelching of our boots. When we stopped for a drink the water in the stream tasted brackish, almost coppery. I swallowed just enough to wet my throat and spat the rest away.

The porters' footprints stretched out ahead in the mud. Get lost here and you might survive a night without dying of exposure. But your mind would go long before your life slipped away. The whole thrust of the place was to intimidate and, if that didn't work, to unhinge. I thought about the man from the Saad Hotel with his bites and his fibrositis ointment. What had he been like before he set off into the mountains? Stolid, down-to-earth, a stranger to hyperbole? Something very odd had happened to him up here. I only hoped it wasn't going to happen to me.

The roots grew fatter, more tangled. Climbing over them entailed swinging yourself over what looked like a giant steeplechase fence and dropping down the other side, often deep into a hole that had been gouged out when the tree above toppled over. The tempest, however, had not materialised. Daniel acknowledged this reluctantly, unwilling to concede that he might have been wrong. 'Tomorrow,' he said doggedly.

We walked on through the afternoon. The valley closed in on either side. The mist grew thicker. Up ahead the porters, all but invisible now, called to one another in low cowed sounding voices. My boots were full of water, my clothes sodden. But I was in a better mood than I'd been for days. For the first time I wondered if this might not be such a disappointment after all.

The camp was under a large overhanging rock. There was sand beneath the overhang, a patch of white amid the muddy green. A hut had been built alongside, but this was in an even worse state than the first one. The door was wedged shut with a stick. Edward opened it and stepped inside.

'Is it habitable?'

'No,' said Edward, his voice muffled.

'Why not?'

'Lack of floor.'

It looked as if the floor had been chopped up for firewood. This wasn't surprising. The wood we had gathered for a fire was so wet we had to squeeze the water out of the moss that covered the bark. After several attempts the fire caught. Thick black smoke belched out from under the rock. There was no discernible warmth, nor any flame to speak of. The wind kept swinging around, blowing the smoke in different directions. As soon as you sat upwind of the fire it would change, entailing a constant shifting round to avoid being choked.

We were sandwiched between clouds. Below us, thin wisps had drifted into the valley, trailing out across the trees. Above the clouds were thicker, standing quite still, poised to drop. Once the fire was lit the porters came and asked if they might have more pills. Again they shuffled silently into line. I gave them two each and a double dose for Daniel and Abraham.

'I don't mind cooking,' said Edward. 'We could have some more tortellini.'

'No.'

'All right then. Tuna ragout.'

We pitched the tent. I settled down to read in the remaining half hour before it got dark. But the rain had got at my books. I spread them out on the sand to dry. One of the porters came over to watch this. His name was Bwambale. He was fifteen and still at school. But his parents were poor, they could no longer afford to pay the school fees. His headmaster had given him two weeks off to come with us. The money he earned from being a porter would enable him to stay at school for another year.

He picked up one of the books. It was *Malice Aforethought* by Francis Iles.

'What is this book about?' he asked.

'It's about a man who murders his wife.'

He laughed. 'Why does he do that?'

'Because she makes him feel very small. And he has fallen in love with another woman.'

'Is it a good book?'

'Oh yes. It's a classic English crime novel.'

'I very much want to improve my English,' he said. 'To read better. Will you help me read this book?'

'If you like.'

I sat down on the sand. Bwambale sat beside me. Edward was bent over the calor gas stove staring into a saucepan. The other porters were huddled round the fire, hugging their knees. The pages at the front of the book had almost disintegrated into papier mâché. I tried to prise them apart with a knife. 'It doesn't matter,' said Bwambale. 'We can start anywhere.'

I started to explain what had gone on so far; how the timid Dr Bickleigh, relentlessly hen-pecked by his wife, had been putting up the tennis net in preparation for a party; how all of Wyvern's Cross was coming to it ('all Wyvern's Cross in fact that counted'); how Dr Bickleigh had first caught sight of the young Madeleine Cranmere, recently moved into the Hall (lain vacant these last five years since Colonel Swincombe's death); how Dr Bickleigh had not been all that impressed with his initial impressions of Miss Cranmere. But all that, of course, would soon change.

Bwambale nodded. He didn't question any of this. I wondered how he would take to the peculiarly English delight in a well-executed murder. As well as being the youngest of the porters, he was also the most dishevelled. His shirt had no buttons or sleeves. His trousers were so thin they were like rice paper. I handed him the book. He stared at the page for a while and then began. 'Dr Bickleigh.' He looked up to make sure he had got the pronunciation right.

'Dr Bickleigh had a habit which he would have rather died than confess to another living soul.'

'Good.'

Bwambale crouched over the book, leaning closer towards it whenever he got to a word he didn't understand. Occasionally he would hand it back to me when he was completely flummoxed, but not often. I lay back and listened to him read about Dr Bickleigh's shameful secret; his 'nocturnal visions' in which he imagined himself lifted from Wyvern's Cross, shorn of all deficiencies and imbued with immense reserves of heroism. A complete unknown selected for England in the deciding match of an Ashes series. 'Edmund Bickleigh 645 not out'. Of being summoned to Buckingham Palace to perform a vital operation on the Queen. 'Arise Lord Bickleigh of Wyvern'. Of Bickleigh winning Wimbledon, the Open Golf Championship and two VCs. Of Bickleigh triumphant.

The porters were preparing their food. Abraham stood ready with the wooden spoon as the cassava flour was about to be poured into the boiling water. The light was failing, the mist white in the tree tops. Bwambale read on, through fantasy after fantasy, until just before sleep Bickleigh came to something new, a plan that would rid him of his pestering wife, remove the humiliation, the constant fear of being shown up. Something remotely practical for a change. Of his wife dying, slowly, conveniently, loaded with misgivings at having treated him so badly. Of course it was only a fantasy, but what if Dr Bickleigh were to take steps to make it happen; to harness his little scheme to reality and make his dream come true?

'For nights and nights,' read Bwambale, his voice faltering now with tiredness. 'He did not play cricket once.'

Eleven

The bog was everywhere. We were on a narrow spit of rock that jutted out from the hillside. In front of us the ground dropped away into an enormous bowl ringed by mountains and topped by low grey cloud. The floor of the bog was an unnaturally bright green, dotted with hummocks 2 or 3 feet high and crowned with sprays of stiff grass. You could smell the bog too, a rich swampy stench that rose in pockets as the ground heaved and belched around us. Daniel was sitting talking to the other porters. When he came over his eyes shone with malaria.

'We have arrived at the bog,' he said. 'There is a path, but most of it is underwater.'

'Ah,' said Edward. 'What do you suggest then?'

'It is simple,' said Daniel. 'We must jump.'

He stepped on to a small rock, swung his arms very deliberately and jumped on to another small rock a few feet away.

I nudged Edward in the ribs. 'What on earth's he doing that for?'

'I'm not too sure,' said Edward.

'We must jump,' repeated Daniel. He pointed out towards the bog, his finger bouncing up and down as he traced a route from one side to the other. Then he looked at us and nodded vigorously.

'Christ, you know I think he means we've got to jump across the hummocks.'

'That's what I think too,' said Edward.

'Try and reason with him. He likes you.'

'What do you mean?'

'He respects your tenacity. Just ask him if there's any other way.'

'Why can't you ask him?'

Daniel's face took on the same habitually worried look it did whenever I came within hailing distance of him. We stood on top of the promontory and looked out over the bog. Mist was snaking its way between the hummocks, blotting out the greenery beneath.

'Would you care for some more pills?'

'No thank you,' he said. 'I am feeling quite well.'

'We wondered if there was any alternative to jumping?' I asked.

He shook his head. 'Jump or go back.'

We walked down the hillside to where the bog began. Bwambale climbed on to the nearest hummock. He turned to me and spread his arms. 'Doctor Bickleigh,' he called out.

The procession set out across the bog. The hummocks were just far enough apart to make each leap touch and go. They wobbled violently whenever you landed on them. Often your feet would slip and you'd be left clinging to the top, grabbing at tufts of grass. It was like being marooned on top of a huge hairy nipple. Again there was no sound. No birdsong, no wind, only the occasional cry whenever anyone fell in. Everybody would stop and lean over from neighbouring hummocks to pull them out of the mud.

After an hour and a half we were in the middle of the bog. All around us the hummocks stretched away to where the mountains met the mire. Daniel called a halt for us to get our breath. We sat down, each perched on top of a hummock. It was only mid-morning, but the light had been growing dimmer for some time. From down the valley claps of thunder rolled up towards us. It began to rain, slowly at first and then in a great deluge, as if the clouds already full to bursting had finally given up the struggle. I could see Daniel, his yellow plaid jacket standing out in the gloom, gazing upwards, vindicated, the rain falling on his forehead.

The porters scrambled to their feet and set off once more, this time with renewed urgency. The thunder grew louder and with it too came forks of lightning that split the clouds with orange flashes. We were jumping almost blind now, not bothering to weigh up the distance between the hummocks, but taking flying leaps at anything that wasn't already occupied. Daniel had sprinted ahead. He was heading for a gap in the mountains, a cleft lined with the same stunted trees hanging with liannas.

The lightning crackled overhead, almost in time with the thunder while the rain soaked the moss and spouted in the puddles. Abraham was ahead of me. The rain had stretched the wool on his crocheted hat. It hung down over his ears in huge flaps, reaching almost to his shoulders. He looked like he was wearing some kind of wimple. The sack on his back was so waterlogged that when he landed on a hummock the weight swinging from behind almost knocked him off again. Daniel was shouting through the trees, a series of high-pitched cries. He was standing halfdraped in a curtain of lichen, pointing up the hill to where a rock hung out over a patch of dry ground.

The porters were sitting round in a semi-circle. All except for one man who sat to one side, shaking his head convulsively. He had fallen into the bog more often than anyone else; from the waist downwards he was covered in mud. No one took any notice of him. But when Daniel joined us he crouched down and started shouting at him, pointing at the other porters and then at the pile of sacks leaning against the back of the rock shelter.

The man carried on shaking his head, not showing any signs of listening to what Daniel was saying. And after Daniel had finished, his tirade rather tailing off for lack of any reaction, the man stayed where he was; his head waggling furiously about, his lips mouthing noiselessly.

'You didn't give that man anything, did you?' said Edward.

'What are you talking about?'

'Pills or anything?'

'No I didn't.'

'I think he might be going mad.'

But Daniel would have none of this. 'Jerome is a very stupid man,' he said. 'That is all. He did not cut good matoke leaves and now his harness is broken. The other porters will have to carry some of his load.'

'Why doesn't he sit still, though?'

'He says he doesn't like it here. That it is a bad place.'

Outside the rain fell in what seemed to be a single sheet, behind which flashes of lightning lit up the bog; sudden glimpses of massed hummocks brushed by banks of cloud. There was some dry wood under the rock. The porters lit a fire and fried peanuts in the largest of the pans, tossing them up into the air to get rid of the chaff.

Perhaps he's right, I thought. Perhaps this really is a bad place. A vast secret laboratory for botanic mutations, where hidden hands laboured to produce the most misshapen growths imaginable. You needed real dedication to come up with things like this; the trees that tried to throttle themselves and the fat spikey groundsels. Nature had turned itself inside out to strive for grotesqueness at every turn. I only knew that I'd never been anywhere so sinister in my life.

'Nut?' said Edward. He was holding out a handful of peanuts, cupped in his palms.

The rain had begun to ease off, gusts blowing across the bog and against the side of the mountains. It looked like a shower curtain spilling off its rail. You could see the rain collapsing in folds as it hit the rock. The thunder boomed away to our left. The porters packed away the pan and swung their sacks back over their heads.

Jerome sat on the ground while all this was going on, not making any move. Daniel had to shout at him, stamping his foot in irritation until Jerome came to, looking around in apparent astonishment and getting groggily to his feet.

Abraham had improvised a harness so that Jerome could carry a partly loaded sack. The rest was divided up among the other porters. Jerome, however, seemed to have forgotten how the harness worked. He stood docilely by, arms hanging at his sides while Abraham adjusted it round his forehead. But when Daniel gave the order to move he fell into line willingly enough, grinning at Edward and me as he went past.

I looked at Osmaston and Pasteur again, this time with misgivings. After the disappointment over the suspension bridge I didn't want any repetition; promises left unfulfilled, hopes artificially lifted.

In the half-light, I could hardly make out the print. It said, 'a steeper and tiresome section leads to an upper bog.'

But even the sections between the bogs had become bogs themselves. The mud sucked at our heels. Whenever you pulled your foot out to take another step it squelched and gurgled in wet possessive kisses. There were no hummocks here to jump to. We had to wade through the most shallow bits of bog, never lingering for too long in case we began to sink. Inside my waterproof trousers sweat was streaming down my legs.

I wished I had the sort of brain that could drop into neutral; my legs still spinning round unhindered by any mental activity. But it wasn't like that. Especially now. No thought or signal, however tiny, was going unrecorded. I couldn't engage any distractions at all. To make matters worse, snatches of those tunes I hated most had become hopelessly stuck in my mind. Long forgotten jingles for carpet shampoo, freak hits sung by school choirs and soap opera stars all fought it out between my ears.

But most insistent of all, trilling away with a cheeriness that was tightening my scalp like a ratchet, came Julie Andrews singing 'A Spoonful of Sugar Helps the Medicine Go Down.' Over and over, the same appalling refrain. Every time I thought I'd got rid of it, back it came, piping through the mufflers: 'In the most deeelightfool way.'

Edward too was humming, an atonal drone through which some kind of melody was struggling to assert itself. It sounded familiar but somehow remote, as if this also had been borne subconsciously from far away. He was hauling himself up on to the banks of a small pond, his knees trying to get some purchase on the wet grass without much success.

'What are you humming?'

'Humming? I don't think I am humming.'

'Yes you are.'

And because I thought there was just a chance this might wipe out Julie Andrews for good, I started to hum the same tune. Edward listened closely as, stationary for a few moments, we both began to subside back into the bog.

'Do you realise you've been humming "What a Friend I Have in Jesus"?'

'Nonsense.' Edward embarked on a few bars to check for himself, stopping suddenly as the realisation sunk in. He sounded genuinely appalled, his voice hollow with shock. 'I don't know what could have come over me.'

It was some time later we heard that Jerome had gone missing.

162

Bwambale ran back, crouched against the rain, to tell us what had happened. They had been making their way through the upper bog when Jerome suddenly headed off on his own towards the edge of the bog, and thence up a steep slope, gaining speed all the time. When Bwambale had got to the top there was no sign of him. Daniel was very annoyed by this. He clenched his fists and walked round in a number of tight little circles, working out what to do.

We should carry on by ourselves, he said. All we had to do was follow the river until we came to a lake. He would meet us there. In the meantime he would go on ahead with Bwambale and try to find Jerome. We had, he said, nothing to worry about. They ran off together, in step as they vanished into the mist.

'I told you that man was going mad,' said Edward.

I said nothing. I knew it was only due to some lucky misrouting that Jerome had gone mad instead of me. Not that it was safe to assume this put me in the clear. Once this sort of thing got started it could spread like fire. Scarcely anyone was exempt. I would have to keep a special look-out for unusual behaviour.

'You know,' said Edward, pulling his foot out of something that looked like an enormous suppurating abscess, 'I can't help thinking this would be a lot easier if I was completely naked.'

That afternoon we continued through the upper bog. I'd been hoping that the vegetation would calm down, that some natural sense of order, even seemliness, would reassert itself. It didn't. Things just got worse. The trees draped in lichen had started to thin out, getting steadily smaller until they were no more than smothered bushes. But what was taking their place didn't count as any improvement.

They looked at first like very clumsy attempts at trees, the kind a child might draw untroubled by any sense of scale. Seldom more than 6 feet high, they had two or three short branches often thicker than the trunks themselves. Stuck at the end of each branch was a small ball of greenery, crowned with the usual cluster of sharp fibrous leaves. They stretched across the hillsides, dotted about in uneasy proximity to one another, like amputated limbs, wedged in the ground and left to sprout. Beneath the trees the ground was covered in thick mustard coloured moss.

It was easier to walk in the river much of the time than alongside it. The rain having dropped off for a while had started up again, with almost as much ferocity as before, peppering the surface of the river and frothing up the stagnant pools. After two hours there was still no sign of any lake.

'We'll find it eventually,' said Edward. 'It doesn't matter.'

'But we could be lost. We could be going in the wrong direction.'

'No we couldn't. We've followed the river. That's what Daniel told us to do.' Edward had stopped and was searching through his rucksack.

'What are you doing?'

'I'm just going to take some photographs.'

'You can't do that now. There's no time. We have to get on.'

'You're getting hysterical,' said Edward. 'You must calm down.'

'How can I? My patience is under immense strain.'

Edward was pointing his camera at one of the trees. By now I could see faces in each of them. Souls in torment, creased in agony, staring back at me from the folds in the bark.

'What sort of tree do you think that is?' asked Edward.

'How should I know? It's just a foul thing that wants to do us terrible harm.'

'Would you mind standing next to it,' he said. 'I want to get some idea of size.'

'I would mind. I'd mind very much. We're on our own in the middle of nowhere. We don't even have a compass.'

'It wouldn't make any difference if we had,' said Edward.

'Why not?'

'Can you read one?'

'I don't think so.'

'No,' said Edward. 'Nor can I.'

Still I couldn't shake the conviction that we were completely lost, that Daniel had abandoned us and we were doomed to wander round and round the bog, perhaps eventually running into Jerome again when we had all reached a similar level of derangement. I was sure we must have missed some vital fork in the river. Now we were making our way up some meandering tributary, miles away from where we were supposed to be, stepping further and further into the unknown.

And then, climbing to the top of a small waterfall, I looked over and saw the lake in front of us. It was encircled by a thick band of mud. At the far end a band of mountains swept almost down to the water. The mountains were much higher than any we'd seen before, their peaks rising out of the clouds, the occasional shaft of sunlight glinting off the snow.

The water in the lake looked quite black. There were no ripples, nothing to disturb the surface. It might have been oil. I wondered if this was the lake where in 1898, S. Bagge's manservant had reported seeing black birds the size of sheep and bellowing like bulls. If there were such things then this had to be the place for them. But right now there were no other signs of life. The shoreline was deserted.

'This is Bukuju Lake,' said Edward. 'It means the place of hostility.'

We began to skirt the lake, wading through the mud. In places it came up to our knees, crinkling in thick brown waves at every stride. Halfway round I saw the entrance to a cave in the rocks just above us. There was what looked to be a narrow path leading off to one side of the cave, also circling the lake but higher up, out of the mud.

This, according to Osmaston and Pasteur, was Cooking Pot Cave, so called because a cooking pot had once been discovered here. Places in the Ruwenzori tended to be named after their dominant characteristics, like Bukuju, or any remotely distinguishing features. In one of the valleys not far to the north was Skull Cave, named by H. A. Osmaston in 1949.

Spending Christmas by himself in the mountains, Osmaston had crawled into a cave and been surprised to see a Huntley & Palmer's biscuit tin lying on the ground. One can imagine his feelings here. A sense of divine intervention perhaps; food parcels raining from heaven in a special Christmas gesture. Opening the tin he had found a human skull inside. The skull was thought to have belonged to either one of two porters who had deserted from a 1932 expedition and later died of exposure. It would seem that another party had found the body, and lacking the facilities for a proper burial had given up their biscuit tin to do the best they could with the head.

We climbed up to the entrance to the cave and stepped inside. There was a smell of burning that grew stronger the further in we went. I saw what I thought were fireflies down near the floor. But as I grew used to the darkness I realised there were three pairs of eyes staring up at me.

'What's the matter?' said Edward.

'There's something in here.'

'You don't have to whisper. What sort of something?'

'How the hell should I know?'

'It's probably Daniel and Jerome. Hello,' said Edward. 'Hello . . . it's us.'

There was no reply. I could just make out three men sitting crosslegged on the ground. To begin with I thought they were naked, but it was only their chests that were bare. In front of them, lying in a pile, were a number of spears.

They made no reaction at all, not moving or speaking. I'd never seen anyone sit so still.

'We're looking for our friends,' I said.

The men continued to stare at us, quite motionless. I began to wonder if they were even alive. If in the absence of any more biscuit tins they hadn't simply been embalmed and left here to deter visitors. Then the man sitting nearest to me raised his arm and pointed at the entrance. He said something, only a sentence or two, but delivered with great emphasis. There was a certain finality about it too, a tone of dismissal. I bowed awkwardly from the waist – due to the lowness of the roof it came out as more of a curtsey – and we backed out of the cave, into the light.

An arc of water was being blown very slowly across the lake, broadening as it went. Coming towards us from round the other side were Daniel, Jerome and another of the porters called David. Jerome looked very sorry for himself, smiling apologetically and half hiding behind Daniel. Apparently Daniel and David had been out looking for him when Jerome had appeared, bearing down on them and shouting wildly.

'Jerome is sick,' said Daniel. 'He has running sickness.'

'What's that?'

Daniel did not find it easy to explain. He turned to Edward. 'Sometimes in Kampala you see people who run. All the time they run. Never stopping. Even at night.' He banged the side of his head with his finger. 'That is what is the matter with Jerome. He needs to go home. David will go with him. You must give them money.'

We paid them off for the days they had worked. I noticed my hands were shivering as I counted out the bills. It had got much colder. David folded the money and slipped it inside his waistband. They had enough food to last them three days.

'And you must give Jerome pills,' said Daniel.

I had the pills to stop our heads from exploding in my rucksack. I wedged the bottle in the top of David's sack. Daniel clapped them both on the shoulder and then they turned and ran quickly down to the side of the lake where the mud was at its deepest. David slowed up almost immediately as the ground sank beneath him. Jerome, on the other hand, still threshing about furiously hardly seemed to notice.

That evening Bwambale read another extract from *Malice Afore-thought*. We were sitting in what was left of Bukuju Hut, a mile to the north of the lake. The hut had no door and a large hole had been punched out of the opposite wall. Most of the floorboards were missing, the gaps between the joists piled high with droppings of some kind.

A few yards away there was another hut in an even worse state. It looked like a derelict privy – sheets of corrugated iron propped haphazardly against one another, nothing much in the way of a roof. The porters were to stay here. We argued about this, albeit without any great conviction. But Daniel was adamant. We should have the better hut.

Edward and I plugged the hole in the wall with towels and pieces of wood. There was a constant draught. It whistled through the hut, rustling the wrappers of the dehydrated goulash we'd laid out by the paraffin cooker. Bwambale came to where the door had once been and knocked on the wall with his fist. There was blood pouring from one of his feet. When he stood still it formed a big puddle all round him. One of his toenails had got snagged on a tree root and been torn half off. It hung down to one side with raw pink flesh showing through beneath.

Most of the porters, Daniel among them, had dug out old pairs of shoes as we got higher and the terrain grew rougher. Bwambale, though, had no shoes. Not that it appeared to bother him much, even now. He put his foot up on a box. Edward got out a bottle of iodine and a pair of tweezers. 'This will hurt,' he warned. He pulled sharply at the nail. It came away with a tearing of skin. I squirted iodine as blood welled over Bwambale's toes.

He gave no sign of feeling anything, not flinching or gasping as the iodine was applied. And when Edward had finished bandaging his toe he swung his leg back down and said, 'Now I would like to read.'

But first there were the porters' pills to be given out. They had gathered outside the hut as Bwambale was having his nail removed, not paying any attention but huddling together against the wind. Abraham, I noticed, was the first forward, with the rest dropping into line behind. He looked rather bashful, as if this was our guilty secret, nothing to do with anyone else's fallibilities. We were running low on Panadol. I'd never imagined they'd be this popular. A few more days and that would be it.

The sun was going down. The last few rays hit the surface of the lake and sent a sudden surge of light up towards the huts, bouncing off the rocks and making everyone shield their eyes. Then the sun dropped further and the lake returned to its customary black sheen.

We lit candles. The flames streamed out and guttered in the draught. Bwambale began to read, picking up as Dr Bickleigh set about his ingenious plan to turn his wife into a morphine addict. Meanwhile, Wyvern's Cross continued to gossip away beneath its thatched roofs and mullioned windows. I felt appallingly homesick as Bwambale read on in a stumbling voice – he was nothing like as fluent tonight. It must have been almost incomprehensible to him, I imagined. To me, though, it was a vision of an England I both knew and had always affected to despise – the orderliness, the complacency, the snobbery, and the odd whiff of homicide to liven things up.

168

It wasn't so very different to where my parents lived. I'd tried to turn my back on it years before, but now my eyes filled with tears at the thought of semi-suburban neatness. I had to busy myself with the cleaning of cutlery to quell what threatened to be a flood. Bwambale had got to the passage where Mrs Bickleigh is warning her husband against Madeleine Cranmere: 'The most dangerous kind of liar there is – the liar who can deceive not only other people, but herself as well.' He sounded bored, his heart wasn't in it. Besides, the candles kept blowing out.

'We can do some more tomorrow,' I said.

I was relieved to hear him stop. It had made me realise that in one respect at least I'd stayed a lot closer to home than I liked to think. Bwambale got up and handed me back the book. I barricaded the entrance with the remains of one of the bunk beds when he had gone.

Edward too, I saw, was reading. He had picked up my copy of *She* and was now flicking through the pages in irritation.

'God, this is a terrible book,' he said.

'What do you mean?'

'It's so boring. All this bombastic nonsense. And childish.'

I felt under attack from all sides. We ate our goulash in silence – not availing ourselves of the psychological advantages of serving the mashed potato in a separate container – and got ready for bed. It was just after half past seven. We took two valium each and crawled into our sleeping bags. This was the second night we'd taken valium to help us sleep. I lay back and waited for them to take effect; the tension draining out of my muscles, my legs feeling as if they were sliding into a tub of warm jelly.

I woke grabbing for my watch. It was ten to two. Outside the wind was rattling the corrugated iron walls. We seemed to be in the middle of a very lazy whirlwind. First one wall would rattle, then another, and another, round and round. Edward was pointing the torch beam at the floor where a large brown vole was sitting eating a Mars bar. He threw one of his boots at it. The vole ran off dragging the Mars bar after it.

Edward switched off the torch. It was pitch black. I could hear him sighing in irritation as he struggled to get comfortable. He thrashed around for a while and then lay still.

'Are you still awake?' he said.

'Yes.'

'Do you know who I am?'

'What?'

'I am X,' he said.

'What are you talking about?'

'I am X.'

'Oh no. Not again. Look, I can't think of anyone whose name begins with X.'

'You must try. Otherwise you'll just brood.'

'Really. I can't.'

'It's not difficult. Have a go.'

I lay in the darkness as the wind changed direction and began tugging at the roof.

'Did you write a series of books about your insatiable appetite for sex and your enjoyment of prostitution?'

'No, I am not Xaviera Hollander, the Happy Hooker.'

'Are you a character in Anthony Powell's novel, *A Dance to the Music of Time*, whose father was a camel jockey?'

'No, I am not X. Trapnel. Anyway, it's not my Christian name that begins with an X. It's my main name.'

'It's two in the morning. Can't we do this in daylight?'

'No,' said Edward. 'I'm X. Who am I?'

'Are you Xenon?'

'No, I'm not. Anyway, who's Xenon?'

'I'm not sure. I think it's a nightclub.'

There was a long pause. It sounded as if more than one vole was now eating our food.

'I just can't think of anyone.'

'Of course you can. For instance, you could ask me if I was one of Achilles' talking horses.'

'I could?'

'If you wanted to, yes.'

'All right then. Are you?'

'No. I am not Xanthus.'

'Why are you doing this to me? I give up. I've had enough.'

Without turning the torch back on Edward threw his other boot at the floor. There was the sound of mass scampering as the voles ran for cover.

'You're not allowed to give up,' he said. 'You've got to keep trying.'

'Leave me alone. I'm going to take another valium.'

'You mustn't. You'll get running sickness like Jerome. I'll give you a clue. My husband's very wise.'

'My husband's very wise? Jesus, what sort of clue is that? I'm getting some more valium.'

'I beg you not to. If you promise not to take more valium I'll tell you my name.'

'Why should I care? It doesn't matter to me. I just want to go back to sleep and forget where I am.'

'You won't be able to. All the time you'll be thinking to yourself, I wonder who X is? It'll drive you crazy.'

'Right. Tell me then. I can't stand this anymore.'

'You want to know?'

'Yes.'

'I am Xanthippe,' said Edward.

'What?'

'I am Xanthippe.'

One of the voles was running around in the saucepan. You could hear its claws scratching on the metal.

'Who the fuck is Xanthippe?'

'Ah,' said Edward. 'Don't you know? She was the wife of Socrates.'

Edward had decided that whatever happened he was going to try and walk on African snow. He asked me if I wanted to go with him and Daniel.

'No.'

'Are you sure?'

'Positive.'

The porters and I would stay put for the day while they climbed up past the snowline. Edward shook out his crampons and poured some tea into the thermos. Globules of undissolved milk swam around on the surface. I watched as he and Daniel set off towards the lake, crossing the bog and heading up the side of a long dark ridge dotted with giant lobelias. Edward looked stooped, leaning on his stick as they began to climb.

It was Sunday. Several of the porters led by Abraham sat round the fire in their hut and sang hymns. They sang in a quiet, almost dreamy way, their heads on one side as they gazed into the smoke. I couldn't recognise any of the hymns, didn't even realise what they were until I saw Abraham making the sign of the cross.

The smoke swirled around the hut. It was barely possible to see from one side of the fire to the other. Outside the temperature was falling steadily, the tufts of marsh grass white with frost. After breakfast of more cassava flour everyone had disappeared off in silence, fanning out from the huts. Round the back, stretching away for some distance between the shrunken trees, there were stiff little florettes of lavatory paper.

Bwambale sat in the corner reading *Malice Aforethought*. Abraham had asked me what the book was about. When I told him his face clouded over with consternation; he looked baffled as much as upset. To choose to read about murder made no sense. I felt stung by his disapproval, avoiding his eye and mumbling along with the hymns as best I could, to show that I wasn't completely beyond redemption. Besides I'd had enough of Doctor Bickleigh by now. We had far too much in common. He had fallen for his own deceptions, had tried to turn his dreams into reality, and look where it had got him – gallows.

I'd looked forward to this, a whole day doing nothing. But now it was here I didn't know what to do. I inched closer to the fire and opened my copy of *She*. 'Suddenly I observed what I had not noticed before, that there was a narrow aperture in the rocky wall. I took up my lamp and examined it; the aperture led to a passage.'

But I couldn't concentrate. It wasn't just the smoke. Edward had been right. It did all seem childish; to hope that there might be anything up here to match the mysteries of the great Kingdom of Kôr. Even so, I couldn't help but find it depressing; living in a world

172

where reality fell so far short of childhood expectations; where there wasn't at least some dim prospect of Shangri-la.

I must have fallen asleep. The next thing I remember was Abraham shaking me by the shoulder and saying, 'Please come, sir. People are here to thief our mountain.'

Outside, six men in climbing gear were standing about, leaning on their ice axes or propped against the groundsels. To one side were their porters, ten of them squatting round a heap of rucksacks. Bwambale and the rest of our porters watched carefully, eyeing them up with deep suspicion. One of the climbers came forward. He had round sores on both his cheeks, almost symmetrically placed like dimples. He and the rest of the climbers were Germans. They had come over the border from Zaire to try and climb Mount Stanley, but had been driven back by the rain and the mist. Now they were going to go walking instead.

'It is very hard,' I said.

'It is not as hard as I expected,' the man said in a disappointed sort of voice. 'But then I got diarrhoea.' He went on to explain that they all had permission to stay here and we would have to move out immediately.

'But we also have permission,' I said.

He smiled and shook his head. He did not want to argue about it, he said, but there really was no possible alternative. They had been told they could stay and that was that. Anyway, he said, there was a regulation that you were only allowed to stay in a hut for one night.

I remembered the certificate we had been given in Kasese. I went into our hut and found it near the bottom of my rucksack, stuck together with damp, the ink quite washed away. Still, it was better than nothing.

I gave it to the man. He looked unimpressed, trying to separate the folds and hold it up to the sky to read the writing. 'This does not say anything,' he said. Abraham had been clicking his tongue in agitation throughout all this. Meanwhile, another of the men had gone into our hut. He came out, blew his nose and spat on the ground.

'This place is a shithole.' He had a very sharp, rasping voice. *'Schitholl.'*

The others too had crowded round the entrance and were looking inside. 'It's full of shit,' said the man, in case the messsage hadn't got across before. Everyone turned and looked at me.

'It's not me,' I said, aware that I was starting to stammer. 'It's . . . it's the voles.'

They carried on staring. By now Abraham and the other porters were looking at me too.

'Anyway,' I said, tentatively at first but gathering confidence. 'If it's such a shithole then why do you want to stay there?'

Rarely have I felt so pleased with myself. The Germans' reaction suggested I had scored a major debating point here, had come up with a splendid rhetorical flourish. Perhaps they were tired or the altitude had slowed up their brains, but they looked flabbergasted by this, unable to muster a decent rejoinder between them.

They all went into a huddle to talk things over, heads bent towards one another, until the man with the sores broke away and announced that they had no desire to cause any trouble and would go elsewhere. I could tell Abraham was greatly impressed; he'd seen an entirely new side of me. So had I. As the Germans got loaded up and prepared to move off I wanted to say, Hold on, I can do a lot better than that. But it wasn't necessary. The trick was done. And under the circumstances I felt that some sort of conciliatory gesture was called for.

'There's a cave not far away,' I said. 'It's dry and sheltered. You could stay there.' The men's faces brightened. They thanked me and asked for directions. I pointed out Cooking Pot Cave. You could just see it from where we stood, a small black hole let into the rock above the black expanse of the lake. There didn't seem much point in telling them what else they might find inside.

Back in the porters' hut more wood was put on the fire and a space cleared for me to sit. 'These people try to thief our mountain,' repeated Abraham. 'But you tell them to go.'

Everyone was very disparaging about the Zairi porters who would only carry 15 kilos per man – as opposed to the 22 kilos that Ugandan porters carried – and were also apt to be fussy about their footwear. We all agreed that 15 kilos per man showed a pathetic lack of stamina. I brought out some raisins and handed them round as the flames licked at the damp moss and the hut once again filled up with smoke.

Towards the end of the afternoon Edward and Daniel returned. Two thin figures making their way across the bog, sticks sloped across their shoulders. Edward looked exhilarated. When he got into the hut he kept walking round, his rucksack still on his back.

'So you walked on African snow?'

'Mmm.'

'What was it like?'

'It was slushy.'

Like the Germans, they had also run into mist and rain. At times visibility was down to a few feet. Daniel had needed to get his bearings. They sheltered behind a stone wall built by the Duke of Abruzzi's party when they camped there in 1906, prior to the first ascent of Mount Stanley. Walking on the glacier proved so hazardous that Daniel insisted they turn back, crevasses were starting to open up around them. Edward had only had his crampons on for a few minutes. None the less, it had been worth it.

'That's something I've always wanted to do,' he said, pacing up and down, his hands plunged in his pockets. 'Because for so long no one thought it could possibly exist. That it had to be a figment of people's imaginations. They couldn't imagine there really was snow in Africa. They thought it was all a mad illusion.'

We ate something that advertised itself as pasta and vegetable Stroganoff – 'large, tasty portions'. It looked like wallpapering paste, erupting in big grey bubbles as it boiled. Afterwards we both took two more valium. Edward fell asleep straightaway.

I lay awake, thinking of Stanley who had mistaken the snow-capped peaks of the Mountains of the Moon for clouds when he first saw them, and waiting for the voles to come out. Later that night it began to hail.

Twelve

I shifted my foot, raking the air for a toehold, and then finding
something gratifyingly solid, able to take my weight. On my left was
a vertical slab of mud. I could smell the wet staleness of the earth
and see the indentations left by the hailstones in the night. A few of
them, white and the size of pearls, had still been embedded in the
mud lower down.

From below Abraham was crying out, 'Be careful, sir. Please.'

'What's the matter?'

'My head.'

'Yes?'

'You are standing on it.'

We were crawling up a long, narrow chute that ran up the cliff-
face like a parting. Trees bent away to either side, the ground
between was glistening and almost bare. Above me, Edward grabbed
for some tree roots, missed and began to slither down, wedging his
arm between two rocks to stop himself falling any further. Above
him, Bwambale was spread-eagled against the mud. The bandage
round his toe, now quite brown, had become unravelled and was
trailing out behind him.

There was no sign of the sun. Our allocation of daylight seemed
even more grudging than usual. Way below, the corrugated iron of
the huts stood grey and unreflecting against the queasy yellow of the
bog. The clouds were very near now, hanging over the top of the
chute and swaying in the few breaths of wind.

The lake had opened out into a huge black pupil, watching our
every move. At any moment I felt the whole landscape could suddenly
flex itself and throw us off. Bwambale was crawling into the cloud.
His head and shoulders began to disappear and finally his bandage
too, as if it was being winched in from above. Edward was next,

growing steadily dimmer until there was nothing left of him but occasional grunts of effort.

Up ahead I could see it quite clearly. A thick white wall where the air turned from clear to opaque, billowing out like sailcloth. I felt that I could hold out my hand and watch it vanish into invisibility. As a child, when I wanted to imagine myself in the Mountains of the Moon, I would swallow hard and feel as though I was being pushed through a membrane. It was like that again now as I stepped forward, watching the clouds close around me.

Immediately it got colder. Drops of moisture settled on my face. The ground sloped away, strewn with boulders, some the size of wardrobes, all crusted with moss so dark it was almost black. Ahead I could see Edward. His feet seemed to have grown to several times their normal size. I realised that his boots, like mine, were swollen with clods of wet earth. He moved slowly, lumberingly, like an astronaut battling through uncertain gravity. There was no sign of Bwambale, nor of Daniel who had led the way up the chute.

I followed Edward down the slope, climbing over boulders, scrabbling at clumps of moss. Abraham had appeared behind me. I'd turned back to see him climb over the top of the chute, as pale and insubstantial looking as the rest of us.

We were going down into a narrow valley, so deep it was more like a ravine. Here, once again, the trees were draped with liannas. If anything they were even thicker than before, tumbling to the ground in great ruched folds. But here too were groundsels, giant lobelias, all the strangest vegetation that we'd seen, herded together for a last furious round of crossbreeding. Branches, thin, black and stripped of leaves, stretched overhead. They looked like the talons of She, just before her final disintegration. The carbuncles on the trees were bigger than ever, enormous bulging lumps covered in matted brown lichen. Everything dripped, a constant drooling that ran down the tree trunks and gathered in pools below. Creepers snaked out towards one another across the fallen trunks of previous mutations, piled high all round and now soft with decay.

I wanted to shout to Edward to stop, to ask him if he had any idea where he was leading us. But I felt that if I opened my mouth too wide cloud vapour would rush down my throat, paralysing my insides. It would be like gulping down liquid nitrogen. So instead I just kept going, all the time thinking of what I had begun to suspect as a child. That while I was immensely keen on the idea of adventure, I had no aptitude whatsoever for it. Even now, I wished I'd been able to thrill to the strangeness all around me, the massed ranks of misshapen things crowding in on all sides. As it was I hurried on, wishing I'd been wearing blinkers.

Daniel, Bwambale and Edward were sitting waiting on a rock, none of them saying anything, each facing in a different direction. Everyone seemed unusually glum. Even Abraham who had pulled up level with me looked out of sorts, half hidden behind the crochet curtains of his hat. I drank some water and handed the bottle round. There were no takers. The pills too, when proffered, drew an equally unenthusiastic response.

I remembered how the porters were known to dislike going too high up the mountains for fear of the bad luck it would bring. They were also superstitious about what they might find. Here at least, little had changed in the hundred years since the Italian explorer Gaetano Casati first saw the peaks of the Ruwenzori. He was told by local tribesmen that no one who attempted to plumb its mysteries ever returned. 'Cold and horrible monsters are said to rule over it,' he noted.

We had reached the end of the ravine. Up ahead there was a wall of scree. It rose up almost sheer into still thicker cloud. When everyone else had arrived – all, I saw, in similarly low spirits – Daniel turned to Edward and me, pointing up the wall of scree. 'That is the way,' he said.

Something worse than alarm – nearer panic – took hold of me. 'No. Come on. Surely not.' I could hear my voice seesawing between octaves. I turned to Edward. 'He must be joking.'

'When have you heard Daniel make a joke?' said Edward quietly. This was true enough. I'd hardly ever seen him smile, except to unhook his lip from the gap in his teeth.

'Last climb,' said Daniel. He still had his thumb jerked upwards. 'After that, all down.'

I didn't believe him. I was awash with suspicion. So much so I no longer cared what he thought of me. 'Do you believe him?' I asked Edward. 'How can we be sure? How can we tell if it's the truth?'

Edward shifted uneasily. Everyone had gone very quiet. After a while Edward said, 'I'm not sure you're well. I think maybe you've got running sickness.'

'Nonsense.'

'You've got a strange look in your eye.'

'What sort of look?'

'Like you're not all there. Vacant.'

He lent over behind me and said to Daniel, 'I think John is sick.' Daniel sat and stared into space for a few moments before coming to have a look at me. I felt as if we were staring at each other down the length of a periscope, from one element to another. He shrugged.

'We must go up,' he said. 'One more time.'

The ground slid and shifted beneath our feet. Stones dropped away, gathering into waves and then clattering on to the rocks below. The wall of scree reared up above us, vast and grey. Patches of snow lay huddled against the rocks. Everything was shrinking. Trees withered away, leaves bunched and curled in on one another. Little white flowers jutted between the crevices, dry and sharp to the touch. Within a few hundred feet almost all the vegetation had disappeared, all but the most pinched and consumptive looking kind, and soon that too had petered out.

The cloud, which had been white when we first climbed into it giving everything the same milky thinness, had now turned grey like the rocks. For the first time the Mountains of the Moon seemed a thoroughly appropriate name for this dead, desolate place, like the surface of a planet the sun seldom reaches, where life has long since been extinguished.

I was having to stop every few paces, wheezing as if I had emphysema. I'd catch my breath and pick another landmark to aim for. But the gaps between rests were getting smaller and smaller; my legs felt like saplings, constantly about to splay out beneath me. It wasn't only exhaustion, though. I couldn't shake this feeling of depression either, of disillusion. Was there nothing miraculous here?

Nothing at all? I'd got used to the absence of the eighty-five copper statues, of Idrisi's Dome and the Garden of Paradise. Even to our failure to find the great Queen herself, still radiant in rayon. But was this really it? I wanted more. It didn't seem that much to ask.

I kept thinking of Speke and Burton. Of how fortunate it had been that the relatively down-to-earth Speke had finally discovered the source of the Nile, rather than Burton who fed far more desperately on the unknown. Burton wouldn't have been able to take the disappointment; to have dreamed for so long and come so far for something that turned out to be a mere geographical feature. A big river flowing out of a bigger lake. What an investment for something so mundane.

For Burton, simply being first would never have been enough. Much greater expectations were at stake. At least he could fall back on feeling thwarted. Out beyond the realms of physical endeavour, bravery, erudition, even sexual appetite where I posed no possible threat of competition, I felt there was the chance of some slim overlap with Burton; in this hope that things just might turn out to be infinitely more mysterious than one had any right to expect.

Something was pushing against my back. I turned to see Daniel, his arm extended.

'You must keep on going,' he said. 'I am helping you.'

Something too was spattering against my face, sharp pellets that stung and then numbed. It had started hailing again. The hailstones came in volleys from the top of the pass, with pauses between just long enough for me to imagine that something up ahead was reloading prior to loosing off another burst of fire.

Daniel's hand stayed between my shoulders. I was torn between wanting to tell him to take it away, that I could manage well enough, and intense gratitude. As I blundered forward propelled from behind, I wondered if there was something wrong with me, if Edward had been right. I was showing ample signs of incapacity, no doubt about that. What's more, I'd been taken aback by the force of my outburst against Daniel, had started feeling steadily more ashamed of myself. At least I wasn't exhibiting the same symptoms as Jerome, but perhaps these came later. And what was the matter with my eyes? I hadn't looked at myself in a mirror for days. I imagined doing so and seeing two empty sockets staring back at me. Moved off, gone elsewhere.

One of the porters was sliding towards me. He had lost his footing on the scree and lay face down, pinioned under his sack, and flailing about like a diver. Daniel stepped out and caught him as he came past, grabbing on to the waistband of his trousers. The sack slewed off to one side. The man had to take his harness off before he could get up. The ties round the top of the sack had come loose. Gazing out of it I could see the enraged orange features of Joe Weider, his Dynamic Carbo-Energiser now disdained by everyone except Bwambale, who seemed to have developed quite a taste for it.

We were getting near the top of the pass. There was a line of crags with a gap in the middle that the clouds hadn't settled into. The ground was getting firmer, the slope levelling out. We walked through the gap and out on to a series of flat rocks that dropped away in tiers.

The hail had stopped, a few last stones falling half heartedly around us. At the same time the cloud lifted, whipped away quite suddenly. We saw we were looking down into a valley hemmed in by rock on all sides and topped with glaciers. Here the moss was quite black, thin doodles on the pale grey rock. It was a completely monochrome world. Down the bottom of the valley where the vegetation started up again, there was another lake, every bit as black and lifeless as the one we had left.

The porters took off their sacks and lay down, breathing heavily.

'Are you all right?' asked Edward.

I didn't say anything. All these inquiries about my state of mind were getting me down. Anyway, how was I supposed to know?

'How are you feeling?' he asked again.

'Fine. I'm feeling fine. All right?'

Edward didn't look at all convinced. I couldn't blame him. I was behaving badly. He was my best friend, evincing genuine concern for me, and I was behaving like a shit.

'I'm sorry,' I said. 'I really am fine.' And then because I felt a certain over-formality might take the edge off my embarrassment I said, 'Thank you for asking.'

'You had me worried,' said Edward. 'I thought you might be cracking up like Jerome.'

'Did you? No, no.' I laughed at the absurdity of such an idea. 'Believe me. I really am OK.'

'John is feeling much better,' Edward told Daniel.

Daniel seemed a little surprised at this, but nodded none the less and said he was pleased. From now on it was mainly downhill. He was sure I would find it easier. There was only one problem. He pointed down to where rocks lay in piles against the bottom of the slopes. 'We must be careful of avalanches,' he said. Apparently they were very frequent round here. It would be best if everyone ran to the lake. 'Is it all right for John?' he asked.

'Oh yes,' I said. 'Perfectly all right.'

We started to run, jumping down the tiers of rocks, slithering on the moss. The cloud had begun to close in again, a roll of grey breakers that spilled over the ridge and chased us down into the valley. The porters went first with Abraham leading while Daniel, Edward and I brought up the rear. The pace wasn't fast. I really had no trouble. And after a while I saw that even Daniel had given up shooting anxious glances at me. Two ducks rose from the lake, furrowing the water and quacking mournfully as they climbed towards us. I realised that they were the first birds I'd seen since we'd been in the mountains. They looked like escapees from another world.

Everything streamed past. The grey of the rocks, the flashes of white where the glaciers swept down to the valley floor. I could see them all blending together, an easy blur through which I ran on, picking up speed all the time. I started to overtake the porters who looked on in astonishment as I sped past. I could hear cries from Daniel telling me to slow down, his voice stretching with alarm, but getting fainter, more plaintive. By then I was already way out in front. By then it was too late. I'd fooled them all. Hoodwinked everyone. And now I knew exactly where I was heading, had spotted it from the moment we set off from the top of the pass. Up high in the rocks to my left, a dark smudge in a fold between two huge buttresses: 'A narrow apperture in the rocky wall.'

It might not look much to anyone else, but I had no doubts. This was it. Vindication. Faith restored. I ran over boulders, outcrops of rock, patches of bog. Everybody else was far behind me, a cluster of dots calling helplessly at my back.

Up a slope now, still gaining, to where the aperture opened out in front of me. I ran inside, through the narrow gap and into a long dark corridor. The air was musty, undisturbed, and seemed to flatten out on either side. On and on down the tunnel until the light from outside grew very dim and I was running almost blind. I thought of Horace C. Holly, beset by ugliness and self-loathing, led blindfold into the caverns of Kôr – 'an eerie sensation, that of being borne into the dead heart of the rock one knew not whither'. So this was where he had been heading.

I could hear drumming, massive blows pulsing through the rock, growing louder, more insistent. Something was all set to happen. I would have to hurry. The light behind had now disappeared completely. But there was another light in front of me, a tiny spot at first but widening out as the drumming grew louder still. And now the air was getting fresher, cooler, blowing up towards me in dry gusts.

The passage opened into a cavern. It was high, vaulted and thronged with people. Soldiers, priests, priestesses, a sizeable slave contingent, all decked out in familiar scripto-epic style. They drew aside as I ran though, straining for the sound of my own footsteps amid the clamour and the drumming. Everyone seemed very excited. They were shaking about inside their costumes, shouting out words of encouragement. At the far end the cavern led on to a terrace. Beyond, falling away all round, was a vast crater encircled by rock. An entire kingdom hidden in the mountain, lost to the world.

There in the middle of the crater surrounded by grass mounds was a copper dome. The light bounced off the dome in shafts that fanned right out across the crater floor. And behind the dome, disappearing off into the distance in single file was a line of statues, so large you had to crane up to see where the water fell, cascading from their mouths in great frothing streams.

There too on the terrace, standing with her back to me, was a figure dressed in some sort of white, faintly shiny material (it had to be rayon). Her back and shoulders were bare, her skin quite unmarked by age. She was gazing out across the crater, shielding her eyes from the glare (it really was very bright). As I got closer she began to turn, the breeze pulling her hair across her face. I knew just what was happening, just who this was. We were being drawn together by Human Magnetism, finally united by fate. It was a big moment for both of us. So the prophecies had been right after all. Mohammad, Homer, Herodotus, Abu el Fadel, Ptolemy, Rider Haggard, the whole crowd, they knew just what they were talking about. It was all true. Every word of it. Everything was just the way it was supposed to be.

Thirteen

There were butterflies all around. So many I could hardly see where I was going. I brushed them away, feeling the whirring of wings against my hands, before stepping on to the tree that ran across the river. On the other side I could see Mr Sampson, leaning against a coral tree laden with red blossoms.

He too was all but hidden behind butterflies. Some had settled on his shoulders, others fluttered round his head. But when he saw us he began to wave excitedly, swinging his arms in huge arcs as if semaphoring to an aircraft. Edward and I ran across the tree trunk. The river below had risen sharply, bushes and branches floated past in the muddy water. Mr Sampson came forward holding out his hand. His teeth were even more stained than I remembered them, practically orange. He pointed at me and cried, 'You have grown a beard.' He looked more closely. 'A beard,' he repeated, so as to reassure himself.

He invited us into his house. The furniture was still covered in sheets of polythene. All had not gone well in our absence, he said. He was still 74,000 bricks short of his quota. He had been working night and day, but the kiln simply wasn't up to it. Now he had begun thinking seriously about building another kiln and running the two in tandem.

We sat down and ate passion fruit, little gusts of soot rising around us. On the back of the door Mr Sampson had written, 'To Aim High and Fail Is No Sin.' Underneath were pinned various charts outlining the rate of brick production. Columns inked in different colours rose and fell across Sellotaped pieces of paper.

'I thought of you,' he said. 'In the evenings especially I would look at the mountains and think of you, up in the clouds.'

He started to tell us of all the news he had heard on the World Service since we had been away. 'There has been a coup,' he said.

'In Haiti, I think, No, surely not another one. I can't remember. Now something has been going on in Surinam . . .'

I couldn't concentrate, could hardly stay awake. All these things had happened to other people, a long way away. When we got up to go he insisted we take some more passion fruit with us. 'The next time you come,' he said, 'you can stay at my hotel.'

We agreed that would be an excellent idea.

'When do you think you will come back?'

'Not for a while,' I said.

Mr Sampson looked unmistakably relieved. 'I hope to be ready in a year, but . . .' He shrugged. 'I can't be one hundred per cent sure.' We left him throwing another sheet of tarpaulin over his latest batch of bricks. The ones on top, I saw, had already begun to crack.

As we walked down to the village people came out of the fields, straggling along behind. We passed a hut where a woman sat in the doorway, her hands clubbed white with leprosy. She was putting bananas into a basket and held out a bunch, calling as we went by.

There was scarcely anything left in the porters' sacks now, apart from cooking pots and pangas. They hung limply from their heads and rattled at every step. Abraham strode out ahead, his feet slapping down on the dried mud. Everyone was keen to get back. Everyone except Daniel, who lagged behind tossing his stick abstractedly from hand to hand. I asked him if he was pleased to be going home. After all, he had wives to see, sermons to preach.

'I must make decisions,' he said. I assumed this meant whether to expand his family still further, but he wouldn't elaborate. Alongside, water rushed down the big V-shaped trough, spilling over the sides, while its wooden supports creaked and juddered under the weight. We came to a row of mud houses on one side of the track. Everyone stopped. There were benches under an awning and people sitting round drinking from plastic mugs. Inside a woman was bent over, stirring the contents of a large metal drum.

'Now we have some tonto,' said Abraham. He was rubbing his hands in anticipation. The woman began ladling the banana beer into more mugs. It was a yellow, watery liquid speckled with what looked like small bugs.

'I will buy the drinks,' I said.

'For how many?' asked the woman, still bent over.

'For everyone.'

The woman looked up, quizzical, the question forming in her eyes. What are you playing at?

This was no time to back down. I wished, though, that I'd kept my mouth shut; hadn't been so eager to play the fatcat, spraying largesse about in return for a few moments' gratitude.

'Everyone,' I said again, with the best show of expansiveness I could manage. Immediately, as if the news had beamed out telepathically, people came in from outside holding their mugs. Through the door I could see figures popping up out of the matoke bushes and sprinting towards the hut – they were coming from all directions. Beakers were raised to me as the drinks were handed out. And, in spite of everything, I was glowing with delight as I gulped back my tonto. It was delicious. One of the best things I had ever tasted. When I had finished a ring of dark brown suds slid down the inside of the cup.

We sat under the awning and paid off the porters, counting out an enormous stack of bills while everyone looked on. Each man then checked his money, flicking through the notes with the speed of bank clerks, before going back in for more tonto. They were only allowed to work as porters once, sometimes twice, a year. In theory, this was to allow the maximum number of people the chance to earn good money. But since it turned out John Matte took a cut out of everyone's wages, it also enabled him to keep his stranglehold on the business as wide as possible.

Bwambale was last. Edward and I had decided to give him enough money to finish his schooling and pay for his textbooks. I also gave him the copy of *Malice Aforethought*, so crinkled with damp and blotted with mould it looked more like a lettuce than a book.

'Doctor Bickleigh,' he murmured, before launching into an effusive round of thanks.

'No, please,' we said. 'It's not necessary.'

Bwambale stopped, uncertain what to do amid all this awkwardness. He nodded, then turned and ran up the hill past one of the mission churches, its white painted corrugated iron spire jutting out above the matoke and the elephant grass.

Abraham took off his hat to say goodbye, enveloping my hands in thick crocheted folds. Daniel said simply that he hoped we had enjoyed ourselves and would come back. I noticed his eyes swerve towards me as the awful thought ran through his mind that I might conceivably take him up on this.

Outside the Mountain Club, two of Matte's youngest children were standing in the dirt, their skin so pocked with ringworm they looked to be wearing chain mail. Matte himself was inside, poring over his ledgers in what little light came in through the door. Edward gave him back the crampons. Matte examined them for any signs of abuse and hung them on the wall.

'Do you want to sign the book?' he asked.

Neither of us could think of anything to write. We sat and stared at the other entries before signing our names and leaving the comment column blank.

The road was 10 miles away. A lorry would be along later to pick up the day's crop of matoke. We could try and hitch a lift. It was, said Matte, lifting his eyes only momentarily from a long line of figures, our best hope.

A priest came by, panting as he walked up the track in a shiny black suit. The sun glinted off his glasses. He wished us good afternoon and then without any further preamble asked me, 'Do you believe in God?'

'Possibly,' I said. Then, 'No.'

'Which one?' He was anxious to know. I couldn't work out if he was wearing bifocals or just had crescents of condensation on his lenses.

'Somewhere between the two.'

'Oh dear,' he said, shaking his head. 'We don't have much time for doubters round here.'

After he'd gone Edward said, 'You should have told that man to fuck off.'

The matoke lorry arrived in a cloud of dust, driven by a Dutch woman missionary. Her hair was frizzed with grey. Her arms, broad and red, stuck out of a faded cotton frock. We were welcome to ride in the lorry, she said, as long as there was room. Two other people were already in the cab with her. We would have to ride in the back.

We helped to load the matoke. There looked to be far more stacked on the grass than the lorry could possibly hold, but the woman was adamant it would all fit. The green bunches rose high above the roof of the cab and bulged out over the wheel arches. We tried to lash the load down, but the ropes wouldn't stretch without being tied together.

One of the men in the cab was very tall and so thin that I assumed he must have AIDS. However, he didn't seem to be in any discomfort and helped throw the matoke into the back energetically enough. Naked except for a loin-cloth knotted on one hip, he must have been almost 6 feet 6 inches tall, but I felt sure I could have picked him up without any trouble. His thighs were hardly thicker than his ankles, his legs tapering sharply away above and below the knees.

'Where do you live?' he asked.

'London.'

'Is that near Portsmouth?'

'Not really.'

Edward and I climbed up on top of the matoke, lying spread-eagled out, clutching on to our bags. The lorry started, turned in a wide circle that had Matte's children rushing for cover, and dropped back down into the ruts. It began to pick up speed, bouncing down the dirt track. The matoke wobbled violently beneath us, about to tip over the side at any moment. The thin man had hauled himself out of the cab, his torso so long and narrow it looked as if he'd been extruded through the window.

'Do you know Portsmouth?' he shouted.

'Vaguely.'

'Naval dockyard still open?'

'As far as I know.'

He slid back inside. The lorry hit a patch of mud. The matoke slewed forward and then back as the wheels regained their grip. We hung on desperately. Up ahead I could see a large group of children in school uniform walking down the track. They drew into the side when they heard the lorry coming, lining the verge. As it went past they pointed at us, sprawled on top, and started screaming with laughter. When I looked back they were still creased up, leaning against one another for support, helpless with mirth.

Nothing had changed at the Margherita Hotel. There were no other guests, the menu was the same, the electricity went off during dinner. Nothing had changed. Or so I thought.

The next morning Edward and I went down to breakfast. It was raining. A goat was sheltering under the porch. The porter ran outside and kicked it away. In the restaurant the five waiters were lined up in their white jackets behind the buffet table, where the cutlery still lay in piles between the pineapples. One of them came to take our order. He was the same man who had been so shocked before when I'd asked for marmalade. We ordered toast and coffee.

It came so quickly, with such a display of attentiveness, that I found the temptation too much.

'I wondered if you had any marmalade?'

This time there was no reaction, bar what I thought was a tremor of extended eye-contact.

'I will go and have a look,' he said.

A few minutes later the double doors to the kitchen swung open and the waiter emerged, bearing a large circular metal tray at shoulder height. On top of the tray was a single, unopened pot of marmalade. He put it down in the centre of the table, clearing a space first and brushing the cloth with his fingers.

I couldn't believe this. It was as if the Grail had finally been placed in front of us. All veils gone, the real thing displayed. We struggled to get the pot opened. The top seemed to have been welded on. At last the vacuum seal was broken and the lid twisted free. The marmalade was a very pale, anaemic green colour. The few tiny slivers of peel looked like worms marooned in aspic.

'What do you want to do today?' asked Edward.

'I don't want to do anything.'

I lay on my bed for hours looking at my boots. They seemed the most tangible proof that we had really been up in the mountains, had covered the ground. I turned them over endlessly in my hands, admiring the scuffing round the toecaps, the way the paint had worn off the copper eyelets. My mind swam about, unable to get a grip on anything. I kept asking myself how I felt. Elated? Relieved? Depressed? But I couldn't come up with an answer. I didn't seem to be feeling anything at all.

Later I went for a walk on the golf course, beating a path through the long grass to where a triangular tin flag on top of a metal pole showed where one of the holes was. Rust had obscured the paintwork and eaten away the edges so that it looked like a tattered battle standard. Gazing up the fairway I could see other tin flags poking stiffly out above the grass, disappearing into the distance as the ground climbed away towards the mountains.

There was a man walking down the other side of the fairway. At first I thought he had a golf bag slung over his back, a lone maniac haunting the greens, still looking for a game. As he got closer I saw that he was a soldier and the golf bag a mortar of some kind. He waved and then veered off to the right into even taller grass, so high that it brushed the shoulders of his combat jacket and all but covered his head.

Back at the hotel I found Moses waiting outside feeding the goat, while the porter stood half crouched under the porch, ready to ward off any further incursions. Moses had come to pick us up. He'd only just arrived after a fourteen-hour drive. Once again there had been robbers about on the road. Moses had, he said, tried to deter them by singing very loudly as he drove through the most dangerous areas. The ploy had worked. He'd made it through unscathed.

'How was it in the mountains?' he asked.

'It was . . . it was wet,' I said.

'And cold?'

'Yes.'

He didn't want to hear any more. He thought we'd been mad to go in the first place. All he wanted was confirmation. I started to explain how he had been wrong about the porters, how they were not only saved but very devout as well. However, Moses wasn't interested in this either. He shook his head dismissively. Whatever faith they had wasn't worth having.

Later in the afternoon we checked out of the Margherita and drove to a game lodge nearby. It was dark when we arrived. A high perimeter fence encircled a cluster of lights. Two men ran out, peered at us through the wire and pulled open the gate. The salt lake at Katwe where Stanley had found the shoreline littered with dead butterflies was only a few miles away. This too was lit up, a ring of searchlights shone on the refinery buildings and gleamed off the piles of salt stacked high all round.

The Queen had come to the game lodge in 1954 with the Duke of Edinburgh on her only trip to Uganda. A special cottage was built for her – the existing rooms were considered unworthy for such guests. Once the Royal Cottage had been a popular holiday spot – you had to book it months in advance. But now few people came. We asked if we could stay there.

It was a pink bungalow with two bedrooms, three bathrooms and a living room. There were photographs of the Queen round the walls, so faded her face and hands had all but vanished. Only the red roses on her dress still showed through. It looked as though the architect, searching desperately for luxurious features to make the royal couple feel at home, had plumped for a surfeit of bathrooms. But there was no hot water and the cold ran out in a slow brownish plait. I sat with the water lapping round my calves, wondering if this was where the Queen had sat soaping herself more than thirty years earlier.

Out the back there was a garden planted with roses and cacti. This had also been laid out for the Queen's visit and was still kept carefully tended. I'd developed terrible catarrh. I spat my way round the garden. The roses were hung with long strings of mucus. I couldn't stop. Every night, before bed, I would go out for a stroll, hawking uncontrollably into the flowerbeds.

In the daytime we went looking for animals. There weren't any. It was a game reserve with scarcely any game in it. For days we drove around scanning the horizon for signs of life. Occasionally we would come across a dried up turd that had our guide on his knees, prodding it futilely for any moisture. All we ever saw was the odd bushbuck that hobbled off into the grass, and hippo. Little else had survived.

The man who ran the reserve, a Doctor of Zoology, told us how in the 1960s he had built up his stock of animals and opened a research unit. His work, on the migrating habits of elephants in particular, was much admired. But then Amin had come to power.

One day the reserve got word that Amin wished to visit. He was bringing some friends with him. They arrived and Amin announced that they intended to go hunting. It was explained, as tactfully as possible, that this was a game reserve, such things were not permitted. It made no difference. The Doctor was told to sit in the presidential Landrover so that he could point out the best places to find game. Over the next few days he had to sit and watch while vast numbers of animals were mown down, many by machine gun. A great banquet was served, of meat from the animals that had been killed. The rest were left to rot. The reserve had never recovered.

For some reason the hippos had been left alone. An old man took us out into the channel between Lake Edward and Lake Albert. He drove a boat like the *African Queen*, almost rectangular, with a canvas canopy draped across wooden struts. Its propellors cut twin whorls in the water as we steamed out into the middle of the channel.

To begin with the hippos stayed submerged. Tiny black eyes, just breaking the surface, watched as the boat came closer. Then they broke all around us, the water foaming, turning white. Heads reared up, their mouths thrown open, little pink tongues lolling inside. More and more of them surfaced. You expected to hear some massed roaring, if not of rage then affirmation. A fitting sound for all these huge gaping throats. But there was nothing except the foaming of the water and the chug of the engine.

That evening there was a barbecue. A goat had been roasted. It hung skewered from chest to tail over the coals, like a greyhound caught in mid-stride. Tables had been placed outside overlooking a dried-up waterhole where elephants had once come to drink. The few guests sat about talking quietly as the chef carved pieces off the goat, one of the waiters standing beside him pointing a torch at the carcass so that he could see what he was doing. There were no candles on the tables. We ate our meal in virtual darkness while inside a selection of Viennese waltzes played in the empty dining room. Moses refused to eat any of the goat. He asked the chef to cook him some matoke. When it came he took one forkful from the thin yellow slab and pushed the rest away.

'We go back to Kampala soon?' he asked. He couldn't keep the hope out of his voice.

'Tomorrow,' said Edward.

After everyone had finished eating two of the waiters came and lifted the remains of the goat off the barbecue and carried it, one either end of the skewer, back into the kitchens. It looked as though they were taking it for a walk.

In the morning we loaded up the truck and Moses climbed in behind the wheel. The man from the reception desk walked over to open the gate in the perimeter fence. Moses put the gearstick into neutral, but kept his foot on the accelerator throughout some lengthy fiddling with the bolt. As the gate swung towards us Moses slammed the pick-up into gear and shot through the gap. The man, hand half-raised ready to wave us goodbye, leaped back instead and flattened himself against the chicken-wire.

We hadn't gone far before it began to rain. It rained the whole day. The ruts on the road filled up with water and the pick-up threw up brown waves as it lurched from side to side. As it got dark the rain grew heavier still. It was so wet even the highwaymen stayed indoors. Nearing Kampala the sky was bright with flashes of lightning.

There were hardly any other vehicles on the road. Moses rubbed away the condensation on the windscreen with his sleeve while the wipers struggled to beat away the downpour. The streets were deserted. But in the centre of town there were four men standing on a roundabout taking down the banner that had advertised the arrival of the Australian evangelists, Cliff and Helen Beard. A solitary streetlamp fizzed and spluttered on the other side of the road. The men rolled up the banner and stuffed it into a canvas bag. From the same bag they took another one, unrolling it and trying to hold it taut as the rain lashed down and the wind tugged at the material. One man was up on a step ladder tying the end of the banner on to a metal frame. Everyone else was clinging on below. I could just make out the wording as we drove past. In big red letters it said, 'Welcome Princess Royal'.

Preparations were already well in hand for the royal visit. Princess Anne was arriving in five days time to inspect various aid projects. There were photographs of her on sale at news vendors, along with the usual pictures of the President and the late King Freddie. The visit was not expected to generate anything like the same excitement as that of Colonel Gaddafi several weeks earlier. Then the streets of Kampala had been packed with people, all straining for a glimpse. This was a more low-key affair, though still worthy of linguistic note. Popular jargon, much favoured by the more radical members of the government, liked to refer to both individuals and groups of people as 'elements'. Thus there were 'pro-people elements', 'anti-social elements' and so on. Princess Anne, in deference to her background, had been dubbed the 'Noble Element'.

I felt vaguely sorry I was going to be missing out on the royal visit – my plane back to England was leaving on the same day the Princess and her party were flying in. But like the Ugandans I couldn't get that worked up. Princess Anne did have a certain air of divine right about her, a kind of immutability that seemed faintly suggestive of the majesty of She, but somehow it just wasn't good enough. And anyway, I'd never felt the same about royalty since that night long ago when the Queen had sped off and left me alone in Trafalgar Square. My own loyalties, of course, were elsewhere. I preferred my monarchs to be immortal, radiant and to bathe in fire. Not in the same narrow tub I had shared.

It was the beginning of Lent. People had smears of ash on their foreheads. The one working set of traffic lights in town had fused. In the restaurant above the Uganda Bookshop I saw Edward's friend Nestor reading a copy of *The Art of French Cuisine*. It was a large book, several inches thick.

He was hoping to do the catering for the royal reception at the British High Commission. There was no doubt that he was a good cook, everyone testified to his ability. But he drank. That was the problem. People would ask him to cater for big dinner parties. Elaborate menus were devised, days spent preparing hors d'oeuvres and puddings. And then on the night of the dinner he would get wildly drunk and never show up.

But today he swore that he hadn't touched a drink in over a month and was in excellent cooking form. Just who was going to be granted the privilege of doing the official catering was eagerly contested. There were various contenders. The wife of one of the British diplomats was known to be keen to supervise the arrangements.

'She will serve tinned pâté if given half a chance,' said Nestor. 'Frozen tinned pâté I expect.'

Much depended on a dinner at the French Embassy for which Nestor was doing the cooking. The British were going to be represented in force. If he distinguished himself there the contract might still be his. Even so, the chances were slim. Later it emerged he'd never really been under serious consideration.

'Do you think pumpkin soup or foie gras to start?' he asked.

'Foie gras.'

'But no one has ever made pumpkin soup in Uganda before. It would be a first.'

'Has anyone made foie gras before?'

He thought about it. 'Doubtful, I admit.'

Hymns were playing over the speakers. Nestor went back to his recipes. I picked up a copy of the Kenyan paper the *Daily Nation* from the table next door. There was an article on how King Solomon's Mines were to be reopened. First worked in the ninth century BC, they had gone out of business two years before when the world market was flooded with gold. Now the price had risen again and mining was to recommence.

The waitress brought two plates of meat stew. It was the only thing on the menu. Nestor scooped up some gravy in his spoon and tilted it forward.

'Look at that. Uncooked flour. Disgusting.'

There was a pink glow spreading across the horizon where dawn was breaking over Lake Victoria. A train heaved its way into Kampala station, rows of office workers in white shirts standing to attention in the cattle trucks. Moses eased the pick-up round a pothole, hooted at a few pedestrians who showed no sign of getting in the way, and headed out west for the airport. Edward had already gone back to sleep, his head resting against the window. Ahead the road rose and fell across the long line of hills towards Entebbe.

We drove past the place where I had seen the boy with the Nile perch on the back of his bicycle and first begun taking notes. Now there were six notebooks carefully wrapped in polythene in my bag. But the damp had got at these too. The ink had run so that my handwriting looked like dim scratchings on parchment, scarcely legible and ringed with watermarks. I didn't know what to do with them. I wasn't going to go back to the British Museum Reading Room, that at least was certain. I wanted to return, notebooks aloft, and say, Hey, remember me, I finally stocked up on some experience and now I'm going to put it to use. I would take my place at one of the long desks and set to, lost in the same glare of concentration as everyone else. The Polish cavalry would be routed at last, their spurs dulled, no longer catching those last few rays of afternoon sun. They'd be gone forever, safely buried beneath huge mounds of rotting turnips.

But somehow I couldn't see it working out. I had a feeling the way would be barred by men in uniform, the memory of my involuntary groans still rumbling in their ears. Instead, I rather suspected that the notebooks were going to stay encased in their polythene, the sealed record of a journey that even now was starting to melt into abstraction.

Moses pulled up to the first of the two roadblocks. Soldiers were still lounging about on the grass, their green gumboots laid out in front of them. We were waved into the side of the road. One of the soldiers told Moses to turn off the engine. He looked at Edward asleep in the passenger seat and at me in the back. For a while we stared at one another, a prolonged spell of neutral eyeballing. Then he looked away and asked Moses if we were going to see the Princess.

'No,' said Moses. 'Why should we want to do that?'

The soldier shrugged. There were a few children along the road, dressed in school uniform and waving paper Union Jacks at every car that went by. We passed under the arch where two carved wooden birds bent towards one another across the road. Flowers had been entwined in the supports and streamers of lavatory paper dangled from the birds' beaks. The second roadblock was up ahead. This was where the two soldiers had rattled my packets of Durex about and told me to love more carefully. It was advice I hadn't even had the opportunity to disregard – the Durex had stayed unbroached in the bottom of my case.

But the soldiers at the second roadblock were now standing in the middle of the road holding their rifles above their heads. In front cars braked hard and began reversing back at speed. Moses exclaimed in alarm and swung the pick-up on to the verge. Edward woke up.

'What's going on?' he asked.

Coming towards us was what looked at first like a dust cloud, moving very fast and fanning out into a broad jetstream behind. As it got closer you could see headlights shining through the dust, shapes materialising behind. The royal motorcade swept by, sirens wailing, horns sounding. A group of police motorcyclists came first followed by a line of black Mercedes Benzes, flags fluttering from their bonnets. There was a blur of darkened glass and then they were gone, roaring into the distance while Moses shouted angrily at another group of police motorcyclists who brought up the rear. They sat crouched over their bikes, faces and goggles caked with dust.

At the airport the reception committee was already going home. A group of ceremonial dancers was climbing into a mini-bus. Drummers were wrapping their drums in rolls of canvas and lashing them to the roof rack. We pulled up alongside.

Moses wished me goodbye. Having explained that he didn't care much for flying, he said he still couldn't help feeling the further I got off the ground the more hope I had of salvation. Edward was standing by the back of the pick-up, scuffing the side of his shoe along the ground.

'Well,' he said. 'I suppose this is it.'

'I suppose it is.'

'Do you think you've got enough material to write a book?'

'No, I wouldn't have thought so.'

'Mmm. There's something I meant to tell you.'

'What is it?'

'I can't remember. It's probably not important. I hate this sort of thing.'

'What sort of thing?'

'Seeing people off. I can never think of what to say.'

'No.'

One of the drummers was having difficulty loading his last drum on to the mini-bus. It fell from the roof rack and bounced on the ground with a loud boom that echoed around the carpark.

'I am X,' said Edward.

'Yes, I know.'

'Who are you?'

'I can't remember.'

'Right. Well, never mind.'

The man was chasing his drum as it ran down the slope towards a line of army jeeps parked along the kerb. The drum appeared to be gaining on him. Edward stuck out his hand.

'Goodbye then.'

'Goodbye.'

He got back in the pick-up. When Moses started the engine a cloud of black smoke shot out of the exhaust as if a huge clot had just worked itself free.

Out on the tarmac two soldiers on their hands and knees were rolling up the red carpet that had been laid out for the royal visitor. They were having trouble rolling it up straight, every few feet it veered off to the left or right and they'd have to unroll it and start again. The luggage had been stacked under the wing of the airplane. Everyone had to identify which was theirs before they were allowed on. It had started to rain, a thin drizzle that spattered on the bags and formed rainbow puddles with the oil on the runway. The stewardesses stood under umbrellas at the bottom of the aircraft steps.

There were hardly any passengers. Across the aisle from me a man

199

crossed himself very deliberately and asked for a glass of water. The plane taxied away from the terminal, picked up speed and took off, climbing out over the lake. I looked down through the window. The vegetation was the same angry green I had noticed on the way in. It looked even brighter from the air.

There was something familiar about the colour. It was only as we were disappearing into the cloud that I remembered what it was. At school, in winter, cough sweets would be handed out every week. They were large green boiled sweets that shone dimly and smelt of eucalyptus. At a given signal the sweets were unwrapped and sucking commenced. They had a sharp acidic taste and for hours afterwards shards of undissolved sugar stuck in your tongue like tiny lances.